Couples Therapy, Multiple Perspectives: In Search of Universal Threads

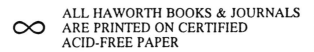

Couples Therapy, Multiple Perspectives: In Search of Universal Threads

Barbara Jo Brothers
Editor

The Haworth Press, Inc.
New York • London • Norwood (Australia)

Couples Therapy, Multiple Perspectives: In Search of Universal Threads has also been published as *Journal of Couples Therapy*, Volume 3, Numbers 2/3, 1992.

The Haworth Press, Inc., 10 Alice Street, Binghamton, NY 13904-1580, USA

Library of Congress Cataloging-in-Publication Data

Couples therapy, multiple perspectives : in search of universal threads / Barbara Jo Brothers, editor
     p. cm.
     "Has also been published as Journal of couples therapy, volume 3, numbers 2/3, 1992"--T.p. verso.
     Includes bibliographical references.
     ISBN 1-56024-374-0 (acid free paper)
     1. Marital psychotherapy. I. Brothers, Barbara, 1940- . II. Journal of couples therapy.
RC488.5.C644 1992   92-32943
616.89'156–dc20   CIP

This book is dedicated to Robert L. Goulding (1917-1992).

Couples Therapy, Multiple Perspectives: In Search of Universal Threads

CONTENTS

ABOUT THE EDITOR

Barbara Jo Brothers, MSW, BCD, a Diplomate in Clinical Social Work, National Association of Social Workers, is in private practice in New Orleans. She received her BA from the University of Texas and her MSW from Tulane University, where she is currently on the faculty. She was editor of *The Newsletter of the American Academy of Psychotherapists* from 1976 to 1985, and was Associate Editor of *Voices: The Art and Science of Psychotherapy* from 1979 to 1989. She has nearly 30 years of experience, in both the public and private sectors, helping people to form skills that will enable them to connect emotionally. The author of numerous articles and book chapters on authenticity in human relating, she has advocated healthy, congruent communication that builds intimacy as opposed to destructive, incongruent communication which blocks intimacy. In addition to her many years of direct work with couples and families, Ms. Brothers had led numerous workshops on teaching communication in families and has also played an integral role in the development of training programs in family therapy for mental health workers throughout the Louisiana state mental health system. She is a board member of the Institute for International Connections, a non-profit organization for cross-cultural professional development, focused on training and cross-cultural exchange with psychotherapists in Russia, republics once part of what used to be the Soviet Union, and other Eastern European countries.

In Memoriam:
Robert L. Goulding 1917-1992:
Pioneer in the Search
for Universal Threads

Barbara Jo Brothers

My old friend Bob Goulding, member of the editorial board of the *Journal of Couples Therapy*, died early in the morning on the eve of Valentine's Day, 1992.

I do not want to write Bob Goulding's obituary.

I am aware that my attitude has nothing to do with reality as we mortals know it; death is as real as life is or so they tell me. Like it or not, it is there to be coped with.

So my dear old friend Bob is gone. I can't believe a personality as distinctive as Bob's was/is could *really* be gone. I think he has to be Somewhere; even if Heaven had not existed before Bob's exit from this world, God would have surely invented it to accommodate such a man. I sound like I am about to deify him, but I am not. He was never my therapist and was my teacher only indirectly. No, I just loved him and respected him deeply, that's all. Little-to-none transference; maximum mutual respect.

This is, you see, what was so remarkable about Bob: the clarity in relationship with him. He had the all-too-rare ability to just "be Bob" with another person. He knew what he liked and what he didn't and he knew how to make clear statements to that effect. I do not mean that he was without flaw; I mean he had that rare ability to own *those* characteristics as well as his virtues–rendering him able to work productively with another person without squandering energy in trying to look like anything but who he was.

Bob, who aptly described himself as being an "expander" rather than a "shrink," brought Eric Berne and Fritz Perls together–first in his living room and then in his practice as he, along with his wife, Mary McClure Goulding–whom he loved dearly–pioneered the use of gestalt therapy techniques and concepts in conjunction with transactional analysis theory. And many, many people trained with him and many, many people received therapy from him.

He went on, along with Mary, to refine this amalgam to create Redecision Therapy as described in *Changing Lives with Redecision Therapy.*

Their earlier book, *The Power is in the Patient* is a testament to Bob's whimsy as well as his wisdom: it features a picture of him on a river bank, fishing.

Reverie

This much I shall return unto the land;
The dust of dreams I dreamed when I was young
And felt the sun of life warm in my hand
And heard the haunting song wild winds have sung.

What may appear to vision as The End
Is but the limit of this human sight
Beyond which all the stars of faith attend
Those travelers who journey into night.

When in the quiet interim I lie,
All mortal things aside, needed no more,
Wrap me in prayer and face me to the sky
And go with love, and gently close the door.

–Robert Lee Brothers (1974)

REFERENCES

Brothers, R.L. (1974). Reverie. *The Lyric, 54,*1.
Goulding, R., & Goulding, M. (1978). *The power is in the patient.* San Francisco, California: TA Press.
Goulding, M., & Goulding, R. (1978) *Changing Lives Through Redecision Therapy.* New York: Brunner/Mazel.

Introduction

Barbara Jo Brothers

This volume addresses the integration of theories, in search of universal threads, asking basic questions: What are the ingredients essential to good relationships; what are the ingredients essential to activity within the particular *psychotherapeutic* relationship; how can what we know regarding psychotherapy be combined to create a whole greater than the sum of its parts?

We begin with the fourth in the series of segments of an interview with Virginia Satir by Sheldon Starr in Virginia's home in Palo Alto in 1985. As she makes her point about all good therapy having the same ingredients, Virginia talks about the vital importance of not demeaning people in the course of therapy. To do so violates the basic premise of creating a safe context for emotional/psychological growth, the very foundation of psychotherapy–and carried out to its logical conclusion, diminishes the humanness of our race proportionately. Such destructive behavior, in effect, throws one more stone in the path of possible progress of human beings learning to live respectfully and in peace with themselves and one another.

Florence Kaslow, who is one of the masters of the art of couples and family therapy, along with her German research associate, Helga Hammerschmidt, takes an in-depth look at the ingredients of successful marriage; what makes marriage work, long term. She asks the experts: those who have produced one. In a pilot study of 20 couples married from 25 to 46 years, the authors seek to tease out those factors that are essential to a long term, successful marriage. With this pilot effort, Dr. Kaslow has launched a series of very important studies which lie close to the heart of the intent of couples therapy in its highest form: to explore the definition of healthy relating between couples rather than focus on pathology. Dr. Kaslow's study will, hopefully, serve to channel future research along these lines, which would produce more hard data on what makes relationships work. In

3

the meantime, the process of replicating the study has begun in Germany by Ms. Hammerschmidt. Stay tuned, as they say.

Joan Atwood, also with an aim toward getting down to the basics, contributes a very well-written article that integrates object relations family therapy with cognitive-behavioral marital counseling into a systemic approach. Atwood's, "Comprehensive Marital Therapy" deals with the how-to-do-it questions, giving very useful guidelines, well documented, drawn from different corners of the literature, and fashioned into a useable whole. This article will be very valuable to the beginning therapist as well as providing a broad view for the advanced practitioner to consider. At the end, she summarizes three general rules for guidelines about the timing of the use of those particular theories in terms of the phases of therapy.

Moving more into specifics, Lynn Pearlmutter discusses structure as a "universal thread" through the beginning, middle, and terminating phases of couples therapy and across the different theoretical models, providing a comprehensive, useful review of the literature on the role of structure in couples work.

Well-known in the field of family therapy, Maurizio Andolfi has also provided an excellent integration of theories including those of Bowen, Framo, and Whitaker. In this substantive article, Dr. Andolfi describes a trigenerational approach to work with couples in crisis. Believing that the issues between the couple cannot be clearly seen outside the context of the entire matrices of the two families represented, he gives a case example of the value of doing family-of-origin work in the initial stages of therapy, showing how even the *initiation* of the process of doing the family-of-origin work became, in the case example, an integral part of the therapy itself.

Steven Heyman's article takes the perspective of Erik Erikson's eight stages of development, giving case examples demonstrating how Erikson's theory may be integrated into work with couples. Use of the eight stages of development model facilitates better understanding of the dynamics of the pair by looking at the current life stages in which the couple is at the time of entry into therapy. Heyman also cites case examples to show how Erik Erikson's theory may be used to understand the two *individual* members of a couple in terms of their experiences in Erikson's eight stages of development as each made their own particular struggle toward maturity that all human beings must make.

George Atkinson, Jr. demonstrates the use of the Myers-Briggs Type Indicator as a therapeutic technique, giving a case illustration to show use of the Myers-Briggs Indicator in reframing perceived reality in such a way that the couple may be motivated toward more emotional openness with each other.

Finally, as a result of their study, Greene and Mabee have come up with some very interesting conclusions which empirically supports the emphasis, in Bowenian theory, on differentiation of self. Their study shows a relationship between differentiation of self and marital adjustment, with the implication that change in the one would have an impact on the other.

These authors have made excellent contributions in the integration of various theories for use in couples therapy, showing the value of the broad view of looking for what works and then, in turn, "what works" when put together with "what else also works." This is the pay off in the search for universal threads: a broader view, a deeper understanding, a richer range of choices–a tapestry of possibilities likelier to include the consideration of *whole persons*, not only a narrow formula limited to addressing one symptom after another.

"All Good Therapy
Has the Same Ingredients":
An Interview with Virginia Satir

Sheldon Starr

[Early in 1985 I asked Virginia Satir if she was willing to be interviewed on videotape concerning her thinking about family therapy at that time and especially with regard to any ideas she might wish to share with the family therapy community. The interview took place on March 15, 1985 at Virginia's home in Menlo Park, California. The transcript of the interview is 60 pages, and this is the *fourth* of a series of segments from that interview covering different themes.]

STARR: Let's move to another issue. Remember when you came to the Family Study Unit at the V.A. about twelve years ago?

SATIR: Uh huh.

STARR: You saw a family and you wrote the paper after it, "When I Meet A Person." That was a very, very impactful session, and you may not remember. But it stuck with me because you had the daughter

Sheldon Starr, PhD, was founder and director for 15 years of the Family Study Unit, a family therapy training and treatment program at the V.A. Medical Center, Palo Alto, CA when this interview was conducted. Dr. Starr is presently Professor of Psychology (part time) at Pacific Graduate School of Psychology and is in private practice, both in Palo Alto, CA. His association with Virginia Satir spanned 25 years, first as student, then as associate and long-time friend. Correspondence may be sent to 801 Welch Road, #209, Palo Alto, CA 94304.

A highly condensed and edited summary of the entire interview appeared in the AFTA Newsletter, Fall 1985 and that version consisted of less than 20% of the interview.

[The use of brackets [ ] and italics are editorial additions for the purpose of clarity and/or emphasis.]

and the mother put their chairs face to face and you introduced them to each other "as if" they were strangers. You introduced them by making comments about who each "really" was, in your perceptions. They were very "moved" and it was very impacting. Now, family systems theorists might say that the session was a very impacting and artistic demonstration of your use of humanistic principles and beliefs [and your charisma] but that's *not* family systems therapy. When it comes to theory, you're not really a "systems" person. I'd like to know what you think about that.

SATIR: Well, first of all, I smile. I smile because most of the time I don't use the language of systems. The basic tenet of "system" means that there is a constant influence going on between all the parts. That's all system means. It doesn't mean anything else, that's all it is. To operate from a non-systemic view is to behave as if things live and breathe by themselves and have no relationship to anything else.

STARR: Well, let's for a minute pretend I am a Strategic therapist.

SATIR: Okay, but tell me what that is. I don't know what that is.

STARR: Oh, those are the . . .

SATIR: Well, I know what it is.

STARR: You know what it is . . .

SATIR: [Impatiently] But wait a minute, wait a minute, let me tell you what I'm saying right now. The word Strategic carries an image.

STARR: That's right.

SATIR: And when I say I don't know what you're talking about, I know that word. I'm very aware of what it means [operationally]. But when you say it, what do you mean when you say it? What's the image you have? Then, I'll tell you.

STARR: Oh, you want me to tell you my image of it?

SATIR: Yeah, because you're talking about it.

STARR: The Strategic therapist is somebody who keeps a pretty good distance between him/her and the family, and they make, see ahhhh . . .

SATIR: How is there any difference in that from the psychoanalytic idea of not getting involved?

STARR: There's not.

SATIR: Then how come you call that Strategic and something else, keeping your distance?

STARR: Okay, Okay. That, I think is the same. If I were [a strategic therapist], I'm trying to be, but I'm not.

SATIR: Good, good, okay, good.

STARR: I'm not a Strategic therapist. But I would say having read what they write, that you're not "thinking" systems, you're over-simplifying the meaning of systems, see? In what you're saying about . . .

SATIR: Okay, let's go back. See, one of the things I love to do is get together with a group of these characters and ask them questions like I'm asking you. See, what I do is I find ordinary kinds of ways and language to [describe] concepts that you would talk about in another kind of way. And so I'm not that interested in the language because it's so dead for one thing, and it never gives me anything. So see, it's very hard for me to talk intelligently about something like this because I *know* all good therapy has the same ingredients. If you're dancing around . . . See, these are only ways of trying to differentiate these different names [therapy approaches] we talked about.

STARR: Differentiate how?

SATIR: Differentiate, who am I.

STARR: Okay, self-differentiation.

SATIR: Yes, self-differentiation in terms of that, but now I'll tell you when it comes to paradox . . .

STARR: Okay, let's go with that.

SATIR: Alright, paradox . . .

STARR: [Attempting to be humorous] A "pair o' docs" is two physicians.

SATIR: Paradox is the following and we all know it when, you do like so [demonstrating], I'm going to show you something and I think you'll uhhh . . . "Shelly, I feel absolutely marvelous." [Spoken with a sad facial expression]. I am showing you a paradox and that's all it is. Okay?

STARR: So why use that word? Why not say contradiction?

SATIR: Exactly, that's my point. That's exactly what is. Now, let's look at that, my understanding and needs about what happened. Gregory [Bateson] used to say that I was one of the only people who knew how to break the double bind. Alright. Paradoxes lead to double bindings. And let me show you how they do. I am saying yes when I feel no. Now, what does the responder have to do? The responder has to choose one or the other. You either respond to this [the non-verbal statement] and say, "Well it's good you don't feel good" when your mouth is saying you feel good (which gets you in trouble); or you say, "You just absolutely look so great" when you can see that [the person does not]. So you're stuck in that kind of thing in which case the responder only is going to move partially. Now, what I do with that kind of thing is to say, "I know that you're doing two things. While you're saying you like something, your head is going this way, and that says to me you come from two [different] positions. And maybe one of them is, you'd like to do that but you shouldn't or you'd like it and you think somebody will be upset or something like that." All we're doing is a differentiation between the conscious part of the one part of our body as compared to another part. That is the dialogue which goes on inside all of us, the shoulds and the "wish-different." That's all it is.

STARR: Yes, that's what you say. Yes, okay.

SATIR: What if somebody else said it?

STARR: That brings up a very important question. I'm involved with training and most of my time goes into that. Let's take the so-called schools of family therapy. The labels seem to be all different and it seems like they change from day-to-day.

SATIR: That's why you have to ask what the message, the image is.

STARR: Yeah, right. Like there's Structural and Strategic and then there's different kinds of Strategic. There's the kind of Milan model where clever paradoxical formulations are devised behind the one way screen by a few professionals who send them into the room for the therapist to execute. What do *you* think of the different schools of family therapy?

SATIR: Well, I only say something very simple. If I have to invent different names for things to give myself differentiation, what does that mean? [I think different names are invented for therapists to feel differentiated.] Alright, to make me feel like I'm somebody I have to invent all these [names]. It'd be like nobody could eat radishes; everybody who sits down at the table would have to invent a new name for it.

STARR: But isn't that part of the reality of peoples' financial backing? Someone who starts a family research program in a University doesn't keep his job too long if he doesn't publish and do something that sounds different and original.

SATIR: Well, see I . . .

STARR: What's a person like that supposed to do?

SATIR: Well, (chuckle) that's a very interesting thing it seems to me. I receive [many] catalogs. I've read them since I was a child, and I notice radishes never disappear from the JC Penny's catalog. I know new varieties are being developed but they still continue to call them radishes. That may be a poor metaphor but what I'm trying to say is I don't think we can make these artificial kinds of distinctions. This knee is going to be a knee no matter what language or in what context you're talking about it. And one of the things I'd like to see is what are the "knee" things that we have in common. I consider that running around behind the one way mirror to figure out a strategy is a different way of modeling for people than if you are standing straight in front of them saying what's going on. Your parents used to disappear. It's called working it out in the bedroom and then you were presented with a conclusion. I happen to believe that I wouldn't want to demean people that way. I'd just share with them what I am going to do. I would like them to have a different experience about getting reality from what they had growing up. It's very interesting; we can call something by a *professional name*, and try to make it look like it's *professional*, but what does it mean when two people are deciding somebody else's welfare behind their back?

STARR: Well, when you figure that way it sounds like an ethical problem.

SATIR: That's exactly the way I look at it.

STARR: You know better what's good for somebody than they do, which if I gather what you're saying, is demeaning to them, and tells them they don't have the capacity for change.

SATIR: Exactly, absolutely, and what really galls me inside and worries me is when the professional, or the office of the professional is used to continue the kind of human behavior that is going towards destructiveness. Now what do I mean by that? I mean that people who are not taught to stand on their own feet [and] to think for themselves, [if we contribute to this], we are adding another bit to what is going on in the world today. I'll make a very strong statement: that anything that I do in relation to you under any kind of power ethos, whatever it may be, doesn't give you the fullest opportunity to learn [the significance of] what you are doing. This *decreases* your opportunity for growing and *increases* your opportunity for destruction, either through capitulation to somebody or attacking. That is the typical kind of thing that happens in families. I read the Nazi holocaust as the extreme. You have to have somebody else in power to tell you what to do because you don't know yourself, and Hitler was charismatic for the German people. My German friends tell me that. Okay, so . . .

STARR: I'm aware that he was hypnotic.

SATIR: Very hypnotic. He absolutely was and it was in a negative way but let's look at that. He epitomized the ultimate in "I know what's best. Jews shouldn't live, so we'll kill them all off." *And anytime that I get a therapeutic theory that behaves as though there cannot be a comradeship between patient and the therapist,* whether it's family or whatever, it is the shades of those [Hitler] kinds of things. Then I would be using my office to help them [patients] to be less than what they could be, which I'm not going to do!

STARR: Okay, the implication then is, at least from your vantage point, that some professionals are compromising their own beliefs or they are not too principled to start with.

SATIR: I will tell you this, it is public knowledge. I was asked to go to France to meet with five hundred family therapists and I became ill and couldn't go. I sent two of my [colleagues to replace me] but that didn't work so they got someone from the Milan group and the feed-back that I received staggered me. They got a woman who wasn't too well known at all and she talked about what she did, and then about these "awful people" [the family in treatment] and she talked about these people in a demeaning way.

STARR: Really?

SATIR: It turned-off an awful lot of people. She talked about this "stupid woman" and that sort of thing. Alright, you see, look, any-thing for me, Shelly, that is demeaning I won't do. Anything that keeps a person from growing, I won't do. Anything that humiliates people, I won't do. I will work every way I can to help people to open up. I will deal with their anger and anxieties and all of that. You can confront in a humiliating way and you can confront in a demeaning way, but you can also confront in a "real way" [with dignity, respect, and congruence] and most of my confronting is like this.

STARR: I want to step back to what you said earlier about strategic therapy. I'm feeling that you overstated your case. Does it really have to be demeaning? For example, suppose I was seeing a couple or even an individual woman who was unable to have orgasms and that was something she was worried about. Why would it be demeaning to say this: "Look, one of the things you could try next time you have sex with your husband is to just tense up every single muscle and see to it that you do everything you can to *not* have an orgasm . . . "

SATIR: Well, I think that would be fine. I do that all the time. Well now, what's happening? What's the underneath part of that?

STARR: The underneath part?

SATIR: Let me tell you, and then you can tell me. The underneath part is that you brought to her attention the fact that she could be in charge of herself. I used this a long time ago whenever I'd get people with tics. Heavens, I used this twenty-five years ago. But I never called it "strategic." If somebody came in with tics and wanted to change, I'd get them "tic-ing" consciously with the way they were tic-ing. At a certain time I would ask them if they could stop and they'd stop. I've been doing this for years. That's only sensible. You do everything you can to bring things to people's awareness. That's not demeaning, because you're helping them to educate themselves.

STARR: Where would you like to see family therapy in the year 2000?

SATIR: Well, first I would like to see family therapists acting like "family" that cared about each other, with each other, and I would hope that we would have begun to develop really good models for what growth is all about. I think family therapy would be small and *family teachers* would be great, and between the two they would focus on prevention and education. We've never done anything to educate people to do anything much. We've done well with cows and pigs and things like that, but not with people. And this marvelous thing we have here called a person, we've hardly touched him in terms of his potential. I would hope a lot would happen in families so that people could help people make their dreams come true, and develop their potential so that kids at two and three would be looked upon as growing in all kinds of marvelous ways. That's where we have to come. You know our birthright is [self] worth: [like] snowflakes–unique. I can see how that [awareness of worth] will be everything. One of the things for me is I turn almost all therapy I do these days *from problems into possibilities. I don't delve much into problems, because I know that if I developed the possibilities, the problems would go away.*

Long Term "Good" Marriages:
The Seemingly Essential Ingredients

Florence W. Kaslow
Helga Hammerschmidt

SUMMARY. Most studies investigating the key factors of a happy or healthy marriage have concentrated on the early stages of family life (Kaslow, 1981, 1982; Lewis, Beavers et al., 1976) and/or provided a general overview of "normal family processes" (Beavers, 1977; Walsh, 1982). Often they do not consider the variables which are associated with satisfaction in marriages of long duration. Therefore, the goal of this article and the study of 20 couples married between 25 and 46 years that is discussed herein is to focus on long-term married couples who chose to stay together after their child rearing and launching years are likely to be over, in order to determine what the essential ingredients are for such longevity. It is hoped that the literature review plus the new material presented herein will help to expand the knowledge base on this topic.

The quest for a meaningful existence in midlife and beyond has many significant features to be considered. Central for many people, perhaps even more than in earlier life cycle stages, is marriage and, as an integral part of that, a satisfying relationship which many perceive as fundamental for a good quality of life and for optimal mental and

Florence W. Kaslow, PhD, is Director of the Florida Couples and Family Institute in West Palm Beach, FL, USA. She is Adjunct Professor of Psychology at Florida Institute of Technology, Melbourne, FL, USA, and Clinical Professor, Department of Psychiatry at Duke University in Durham, NC, USA. From 1987-1990 she served as the first President of the International Family Therapy Association.

Helga Hammerschmidt, MA, is a psychologist researcher from Munich, Germany who engages independently in research projects as an investigator and consultant.

Funding for this research project was provided by the Florida Couples & Family Institute.

physical health. Yet, as Walsh pointed out (1980), in popular film depictions of adults in their later years prior to that time, each film "reflects and fosters a growing sensitivity to *a person* who is attempting, with courage and daring, to adapt to losses and challenges of later life in ways that fit needs for self identity, satisfying companionship, and meaningful experience." She adds that none of these films provide options for healthy later life adjustments within *a family* context; rather each hero or heroine is marginal to or has no family, is widowed, and often becomes somewhat deviant. Pessimism about and dread of old age dominate. Unfortunately, these portrayals represented and perpetuated widely held stereotypes.

In the 1980s a tender portrayal of mature, sensitive adult love that dealt with enduring compassion in a marital dyad was brought to the screen in *On Golden Pond*. Although the sense of losses experienced was a dominant theme, it was wistfully balanced by some focus on intact capacities and reciprocal caring. Such a compassionate and touching depiction of older couples remains atypical in the mass media.

There is a tendency to think of those who pass their silver anniversary together and continue beyond toward the golden celebration as the young elderly. Yet some of these couples are in the mid to late forties, and many are in their fifties or early sixties. If they are physically and emotionally healthy during these *middle* years of their lives, they may be quite expansive. Rather than experiencing multiple losses or a noticeable decline they may be taking on new and challenging career responsibilities, avidly pursuing hobbies or cultural activities like painting or sculpting, playing in an orchestra, or acting in a theatre company; participating in aerobics or jazzercise classes; jogging, playing tennis or golf, sailing or motor boating, fishing or skiing, travelling, or writing books and articles. Many couples in the 50 to 70 year age bracket are active, contributing members of their families, the workaday world, and their communities. Movie portrayals of them as sad, widowed or divorced, marginal, pessimistic and alienated do not mirror the reality of the many vibrant, optimistic, long term married couples who currently enjoy their lives.

With a sizeable increase in predictable longevity, the percentage of the population in the 50-plus age group in our society is mounting rapidly and it is important that we augment our knowledge about fulfilling behaviors and relationships in this stage of the life cycle–the middle years and beyond. It is hoped that the review of pertinent literature and the results of the *pilot* study described herein will help guide therapists and lay people in knowing which behaviors and attitudes are conducive to long term, "good," satisfying marriages. In addition, it is hoped that it will generate additional research that includes populations characterized by other demographic variables and that are longitudinal as well as cross sectional in design.

In this article a theoretical framework on healthy individuals and families is presented first. This is followed by a review of the literature and a discussion of salient concepts. The third section presents the data derived from a study of 20 couples married 25 to 46 years. The final portion of the paper attempts to integrate the portrait of healthy individuals and couples and the highlights of the literature survey with the study findings based on self-report data.

THEORETICAL FRAMEWORK

Maslow, in his philosophic treatise "Toward a Psychology of Being" (1962) focused on the healthy personality and identified this type of person as having many more B, or *being* needs, than D, or *deficit* needs. He or she is likely to be creative, to be willing to take some risks and be adventuresome, to think independently and function autonomously, to have a good sense of humor and a grasp of the absurdity of life, to be able to make commitments to projects undertaken and to meaningful interpersonal relationships; in sum, to be *self actualizing* and, by implication, to foster this quality in others.

Friedman (1987) appears to be describing the same type of individual in his more recent depiction, in the form of twelve principles, of the High Well Being (HWB) person. A condensation of his portrait follows.

THE CORE PRINCIPLES OF WELL-BEING

High Well Being (HWB) persons:

1. Develop a clarity in regard to the meaning, direction and purpose in their lives and develop a vision so they can attain their purpose. They set goals consistent with this purpose and vision.

2. Perceive themselves as creators rather than reactors to circumstances. They creatively choose and decide what they want in alignment with their sense of meaning, direction and purpose in life.
3. Develop a positive, optimistic and forgiving attitude. They look on the bright side of things. They think optimistically about themselves, other people and events. They tend not to hold onto grievances against themselves and others.
4. Develop an ability to take a situation that initially may look unfortunate or unpleasant and reperceive or reframe their experience of it in a more useful, helpful and constructive way.
5. Develop ability to generate creative alternatives, possibilities, options and solutions to perceived problems or difficulties. Consequently, they are flexible and open-minded.
6. As a result of applying the previous 5 principles, develop a sense of accomplishment in their personal and professional lives, and a satisfaction with their personal growth.
7. Develop a high sense of self-esteem, self-value, self confidence and self-love. They know they must value, respect, appreciate and love themselves in order to be able to value, respect, appreciate and love others.
8. Allow themselves opportunities to tap into the inner source of security, peace, joy and strength. As a result of valuing, respecting and loving themselves, they feel secure, and accept themselves for who they are, as an individual with unique talents, abilities, skills and interests.
9. Generally develop loving, intimate relationships with a spouse or lover. Because they love and appreciate themselves, they are willing and able to love and appreciate another. They share themselves, listen, support and encourage another in an intimate relationship.
10. Develop caring, close friendships. These friendships can be with members of the same and/or opposite sex. Respecting themselves, they can respect others. Caring for themselves, they can give to others. They intuitively know that what they give is what they will receive.
11. Have a sense of gratitude for what they have attained and received in life. Although they are often busy creating new re-

sults and accomplishments, they also have a deep sense of appreciation and thankfulness for what they already have received and can acknowledge this.

12. Frequently have some kind of intuitive connection with a universal Source, Center or Higher Self. They have the ability to tap into or access this higher wisdom or creative intelligence within them. For many people it is this strong connection with a universal Source, Center or Self that generates their sense of meaning, direction, purpose and vision in life.

When emotionally healthy individuals marry, they are apt (perhaps even destined) to gravitate toward and select another healthy person, for, as Bowen indicated, we choose someone at the same level of individuation from the family of origin (Bowen, 1978). In my clinical and research work I (F.K.) have repeatedly found that this translates into the fact that individuals select someone at approximately the same level of emotional health and maturity as they are and that this factor invariably constitutes a major, even if a somewhat unconscious, aspect of the basis for a strong, positive attraction. It is from the unions of two healthy, high well being adults that healthy families evolve.

At a 1990 conference devoted to the theme of the healthy family (Family Therapy News, 1990), participating researchers, clinicians and theoreticians indicated that a consensus had emerged about nine characteristics that seem to constitute the *"basic dimensions of a strong, healthy family."* They were delineated as:

1. *Adaptive ability:* This refers to the family's ability to adapt to predictable life cycle changes as well as to stressful events . . . Such abilities are related to external resources as well as good communication and other internal family processes.

2. *Commitment to family:* This involves both the recognition of individual worth and acceptance of the value of the family as a unit.

3. *Communication:* This refers to clear, open, and frequent communication patterns.

4. *Encouragement of individuals:* This refers to the family's ability to encourage a sense of belonging at the same time individual development is encouraged.

5. *Expression of appreciation:* This refers to doing things consistently that are positive for the other person simply for their sake (referred to elsewhere as "volunteering"). The presence of a sense of "delight" and related feelings shared by family members was emphasized.

6. *Religious/spiritual orientation:* Many researchers describe religiosity or *spirituality* as a characteristic of healthy families, although there is no consensus regarding the particular aspects of spirituality that are important to functioning.

7. *Social connectedness:* This refers to a connection with the larger society–extended family, friends, and neighbors, and participation in community activities–which typically makes available external resources to assist a family in adapting and coping.

8. *Clear roles:* This refers to a clear and flexible role structure in which family members know their roles and responsibilities and thus are able to function effectively in times of crisis as well as during normal times.

9. *Shared time:* This refers to the sharing of both quality and quantity time by family members to the degree to which this is enjoyable for them.

Some of these ideas are drawn from the work of Olson and his colleagues on the circumplex model (1990; Olson and Portner, 1983; Olson, Russell and Sprinkle, 1983) in which the centrality of adaptability/flexibility, closeness and cohesion, and good problem solving and communication skills are highlighted. Others are predicated, at least partially, on the contributions of Beavers and his colleagues, in their continually evolving typology of healthy (optimally functional), mid-range and dysfunctional families (Lewis, Beavers, Gossett and Phillips, 1976; Beavers, 1977, 1982). Their work particularly illuminates the fact that healthy families are open systems–i.e., in the above criteria–maintain social connections to the extended family and larger work and play communities, and that they have a transcendental value system–a system of meaning and value that is often derived from and expressed through a religious/spiritual orientation in life. A characteristic of healthy families not mentioned in the above list, but cited by others, is that they have clear boundaries between the generations, so that no intimate sexual contact occurs across generations and children are not parentified; and between people; that is, they respect the privacy of one another (Minuchin, 1984; Kaslow, 1981, 1982) and are neither prying nor intrusive.

MARITAL SATISFACTION AND DISSATISFACTION

Satisfaction in close relationships has been a frequent topic of research in the social psychology and behavioral marital therapy literature (see, for example, Fincham, 1991; and Jacobson and Margolin, 1979, for reviews of this literature). The concept of satisfaction is inherently a very subjective one; only the individuals involved can assess their own level of satisfaction in a relationship. The desires and expectations each party has are salient; in addition, the agreement of the couple about what constitutes happiness for them is vital. Satisfaction entails having one's fundamental needs and desires met, as well as fulfilling what one's spouse wants from them, i.e., can they both give to and take from one another in an easy, spontaneous, willing manner (Sager, 1976). Satisfaction implies a sense of well being, contentment and overall good feeling, including comraderie, affection and safety.

Such a definition of satisfaction is broad enough to permit multi-cultural comparisons and to be applicable to all kinds of "mixed marriages." A narrow definition is not acceptable since different couples perceive of satisfaction in quite different ways and require different levels of depth to achieve this. Often "harmonious" and "happy" are used synonymously for "satisfying." Perhaps satisfaction connotes a little less excitement than happiness, but it may reflect more safety and intimacy. The concept of a healthy marriage as it was articulated in *Portrait of the Healthy Couple* depicts an ideal perception of conjugal relationships (Kaslow, 1982) and illuminates many of the same characteristics found in healthy families alluded to earlier. Some couples with less expectations also are apt to describe their marriages as satisfying–couched more in terms of "I have nothing to complain about, my spouse is not abusive, does not cheat and/or is not alcoholic." They do not aspire to peak experiences, exuberant interactions, and hedonistic moments or profound shared tranquility.

The relationship of mid-range couples is neither good nor bad. They also experience less satisfaction. They are more "normal," a term that conveys average, and the average couple falls close to the mid-range category on a curve of normal distribution. However, mid-range couples are often more conservative and less adventuresome than healthy couples and lack their vitality, openness and search for new experiences.

In dysfunctional families, of both the chaotic and enmeshed categories, satisfaction is low and conflict is high. The probability that children will become symptomatic is strong. Cohesion, flexibility and adequate supervision are often lacking—rules and clear role expectations are either lacking or too rigid, and the concept of having fun together is negligible.

When a couple remains together, it does not necessarily mean that they have a good relationship. One or both parties may abhor the idea of divorce; it may be contrary to their religion. They may fear loneliness, change, freedom, self sufficiency. Something and someone—even if boring, dull, grumpy, demanding, sarcastic, verbally abusive, and/or non-communicative—may be preferable to nothing and no one. Being married and part of a couple is familiar and may be less fraught with anxiety than being single. They may drift along—aware of a vague discontent that occasionally flares up and leads to a critical confrontation, but neither wants to disrupt the marriage and/or the nuclear and extended family relationships (Kaslow and Schwartz, 1987). And the thought of dividing the assets can be overwhelming (Weitzman, 1985). For decades most couples plan and save for their future together—when that future arrives they do not want to part with the dream of enjoying their later years together. So they stay together, living "as if" the marriage is fulfilling or in an uneasy truce.

No marriage can be constantly happy throughout the years. Each partner's personal development, the rearing and launching of the children, the loss of parents and perhaps of job, illnesses and accidents, changes in financial status, and the normal vicissitudes of life necessitate continual adaptation of each partner individually and as a couple unit. One mate's growth can be distressing to the other, particularly if it leads to some separate and exciting journeys, or it can prove exhilarating for both if it stimulates the enjoyment of new horizons.

Schwarzenauer (1980) found that the satisfaction of wives is relatively low when the children are small. Husbands reported the lowest satisfaction after seven years of marriage and in the period before retirement.

Schwarzenauer and Baur (1976) found a correlation between ego strength of the wives and marital harmony. The greater her ego strength, the higher the level of marital accord. This is consistent with earlier hypothesizing that runs through the family sociology literature that emotional stability in each of the partners is essential for a solid relationship. Conversely, marriages in which one or both are distressed or dysfunctional are rarely marked by a high level of mutual satisfaction. Rather the "neurotic," "psychotic" or "borderline" person is rarely at ease with him or herself or with anyone else. His or her level of anxiety, uncertainty, and internal stress is too high to permit relaxed, enjoyable work-related or social transactions, including intimate marital relationships (Kaslow, 1982). Bowlby (1975) calls such relationships anxiety-attachments (from angst bindungen–our translation); today one genre of such dyads are frequently labeled co-dependent relationships.

Willi (1975, 1982) described various causes of marital dysfunction and what the most appropriate interventions are to use with each of four patterned interactions. His core concept is "collusion," a word he uses to refer to the unconscious interplay between spouses based on similar, unresolved central conflicts. He perceives a couple's relationship as a system in which the spouses' behaviors are both determined by personal history and their mutual interdependence. Using a psychodynamic framework, he stresses that both hope to overcome past traumatizations and conflicts through what they derive from the marital interaction. In their "joint defense agreement" they both enhance their partnership by polarizing into complementary roles . . . One mate seeks resolution through progressive behavior; the other through regressive behavior. (An example of this is when the woman is an adult survivor of an incestuous relationship, the memory of which resurfaces after marriage. For her this needs to be worked through before she can engage in a sexually active and gratifying relationship with her husband. He, in turn, wants her to "let go of the past and indulge in mutual sexual pleasuring." If he comes from a physically abusive background and becomes threatening to her before he learns how to handle his anger and frustration in non-violent ways, an emotional volcano can erupt at any time.) When their common defense alliance collapses, which it almost always does, the disillusionment precipitates serious marital crises.

CHILDREN'S DEPARTURE–TEMPORARY AND/OR PERMANENT

Clinically many therapists see couples who have stayed together *"for the sake of the children."* Since the children are the major raison d'etre for the continuity of the marriage, one or both of the parents may attempt to and succeed in delaying the completion of the young adult child's (children) leaving home (Haley, 1980). Their offspring may collude, not only because home is comfortable and because living there is much more financially manageable, but also because they know or sense that their parents' marriage will split asunder if they must live alone together in an "empty nest" (Neugarten, 1970), or that one parent will be unable to tolerate the separation from a child to whom he or she is overly attached. They recognize that the spousal connection is weak, that it is mainly the parental ties that bind them together because they have been unable to nurture, expand and transform their marital bond over time.

Since the 1960s many young adults have sought to leave home by going away to college or to take a job, not waiting until they married to set up their own living quarters. They pursued their independence and had no intention of returning to live in their parents' home again. Parents have been chastised for clinging to young adult children and have been encouraged instead to help them to individuate. For many mothers, the departure of the youngest child heralded new freedom for her to avidly pursue her own separate goals–at last she was free to go back to college, to put more time into building a career, expanding her volunteer activities and/or her sports or artistic endeavors. If she could let go and not hover unhappily around her "empty nest," she could embark on creating new opportunities and respond to new challenges.

Likewise, there are usually fewer demands on a father's time to be available for adolescents' activities and once the youngsters leave home. And as the weight of financial responsibility for the children's costly education, food, clothing, and activities diminish, many couples have more time to spend together that is adult rather than child centered, and more funds available to spend on their own pleasures, unless they have fostered prolonged financial dependency.

Sometimes the series of changes caused by the young adult's appropriate departure at this developmental/transitional stage of his or her life cycle triggers a chain of perturbations in the parents' marriage. Many marriages cannot survive the absence of children, and divorce occurs at the 25 year mark and beyond. These couples differ from those in our study in that they are not willing or able to transform their relationship into a more satisfying union after the children depart. One or both want something different than their marriage provides and believe that, like their children, they have to leave the family nest and embark on a new life in order to restore their sense of *self worth* and to create what they desire in life.

A new phenomenon emerged in the latter half of the 1980s, and is continuing into the 1990s. It is the trend toward young adult family members returning home of their own volition, often to the consternation of one or both parents who were looking forward to this period of time alone together after several decades of active daily parenting. When children decide to return home after completing college, losing a job, getting a divorce, or becoming financially overextended, the parents may no longer like the idea of a "crowded nest." This unplanned for return of a young adult child can place financial and emotional pressure on the marital pair–particularly if they do not agree as to (1) whether to permit the child to return home, (2) what costs they are willing to absorb for their adult child's support, and (3) what the "rules and regulations" circumscribing the living together again will be. But for the most part in the United States today, by the time a couple are married for 30 years, the children, if not severely impaired physically or emotionally, are no longer living in the parents' residence.

What helps couples to get through all the usual life cycle transitions and traumatic events? What philosophy of life, personal qualities and coping skills enable them to resume a satisfying, fulfilling partnership or to enrich it further after serious crises have disrupted a rather good equilibrium? We will address some of these queries below in the reporting and interpretation of the study data.

STUDY OF LONG TERM MARRIED COUPLES

Purpose

The goals of this study were to explore the characteristics of long term marriages and discern which variables are most likely to contribute to a satisfying, "healthy," relationship in the middle and later stages of the life cycle. It was intended to be a *pilot* study that might be extended in future studies.

Methodology

Questionnaires and rating scales were sent to 63 couples. The original sample was comprised of long term married couples whose names had been collected by the first author and her then associate, Timothy Rot, Psy.D., from individuals to whom they had mentioned the study. Colleagues all over the country were asked for recommendations of possible respondents who met the single criteria of *length of marriage*. Some subjects who received the questionnaire contacted the first author to suggest acquaintances who they thought would be willing to respond. A networking approach was the methodology used to put together the potential study population from a variety of states in this country.

Each couple received duplicates of all forms–A for the wife and B for the husband–of a questionnaire specifically constructed for this study and a combination of the Dyadic Adjustment Scale (Spanier, 1982), and two items from the Marital Adjustment Test (Locke and Wallace, 1959). To investigate the factors the respondents believed contributed to the longevity of their marriages, preference was given to open-ended answers rather than a checklist. In this effort to obtain spontaneous, more meaningful and personal answers, drawing on respondents' perceptions, we possibly lost some information and/or uniformity of answers. Sociodemographic data and history of parents' marriage were solicited. They were instructed to each respond totally separately and to only discuss their reactions and responses with one another, if they chose to do so, after completing the forms. We do not know to what extent these instructions were followed. However, several reported later to the principal investigator that the discussions had proven illuminating and fruitful and that they were pleased with the congruence of their responses, indicating that they had abided by the guidelines regarding timing. (This was reported voluntarily by 4 of the couples who scored in the satisfied category.)

Description of the Sample

In this pilot study we had useable returns from 20 couples. All were Caucasian; the majority were of upper middle and lower upper socio-economic status. Joint incomes of over $51,000 per year were reported by 17 of the 20 couples, with 14 of the 20 falling in the $101,000 per year income bracket. Thus almost all seem to have achieved a high standard of living and to be relatively affluent. They were married between 25 and 46 years, with a mean of 35.6 years. For two men and one woman, these were second marriages. Nineteen couples have had children. Only four couples still had children living at home. In age the women ranged from 46 to 71 years, with a mean of 59; the men ranged from 49 to 74 years of age, with a mean of 62.1.

In terms of *religious orientation,* in 19 of the 20 couples the partners were raised in the same religion. Three-quarters were Jewish, the rest were Protestant and Catholic. One wife was Greek Orthodox.

In terms of *educational background,* everyone had completed "high school" and all but 3 women and 2 men of the 40 respondents had gone on to higher education. Three women and one man checked "some college." Four women and 7 men completed undergraduate colleges or universities. One woman and 2 men had done some postgraduate work. Three women and one man had masters degrees. A large percentage of respondents held some form of doctoral degree. For the women–there was one J.D., one M.D., one D.Min., and three Ph.D's. Of the men–one M.D. and six Ph.D's had been earned. Thus our sample is comprised of an extremely well educated group of subjects.

Only one couple had already retired. In the 19 other couples, all of the men and 18 of the women were still gainfully employed. All of the men were in relatively high level business, professional and executive positions. Of the 18 women working–two were in secretarial positions, the remainder were also in prestigious and remunerative business, professional and executive positions. Thus a picture of similarity of educational and occupational level within couples emerged in this sample.

Because of the relatively small sample, there are limits to the generalizability of the data. The findings are likely to be most applicable to well educated, financially successful couples who have a strong work ethic and a religious affiliation.

It is hypothesized that the low return rate (31.5%) was attributable to the following factors:

1. The sensitive, personal nature of the questions asked;
2. The busyness of the high functioning people in the total potential study population;
3. The length of time needed to complete the Questionnaire and the Inventory (between 1 and 1-1/2 hours);
4. The discomfort the questions may have aroused in couples who were not satisfied with their current marital interaction and therefore opted not to participate.

Study Results

One benefit of the relatively small sample size is that it permitted a detailed analysis of the data, most of which follows.

The 20 responding couples were divided into three categories–satisfied, mid-range, and not satisfied. The cut-off points were established using Spanier's scoring system on the dyadic adjustment scale (DAS) (1976). The mean satisfaction score in Spanier's study population of over 700 couples was 40.5. Thus, the 10 couples who scored between 41 and 48 were placed in the satisfied group. Their total scores on the DAS fell between 120 and 136. Thus, both members of such couple had a mean score which was well above the total DAS for Spanier's study group, which was 114.8.

The mid-range couples scored between 37 and 40 on the satisfaction scale and 109 to 119 on the total DAS, respectively. The non-satisfied couples scored between 32 and 36 on the satisfaction scale and 101 to 108 on their total DAS, with only one exception, noted below.

One factor we noted was the amount of variance between the partners' responses. In the satisfied group there was great consistency in level of satisfaction and on overall score. In the mid-range couples, more differences appeared. Where the difference was great, for example, with the one couple who scored 110 vs. 134, with one expressing great discontent and the other rating the marriage as excellent, we classified them as a dissatisfied couple.

Comparing the three groups of 10 satisfied, 4 mid-range, and 6 unsatisfied couples we found some actual although not statistically significant differences in the variables attributed to the longevity of marriage. Love, mutual respect and trust, shared interests and value system, shared love for children, the ability to give and take, and flexibility were all mentioned much more frequently by satisfied couples, less so by mid-range pairs, and least by unsatisfied couples.

Sensitivity to the needs of one's spouse appears only in the group of satisfied (30%). An equalitarian relationship with many complementary features was also cited as important by satisfied couples, but less frequently than the factors cited earlier.

Interestingly, having and sharing interest in their children was cited by all as important in their lives together, but *only* by unsatisfied couples as a reason for the longevity of their marriages (33% of this group). The satisfied group stayed together because they wanted to be with each other, and not for the sake of the children. The dissatisfied group also disclosed that they experienced a lack of affectional expressiveness and support from one another. The mid-range couples revealed a deficit in the arena of "good communication."

Fun, humor and playfulness rarely appear as factors in the responses to the mid-range and unsatisfied couples, i.e., these do not seem to be a vital part of their lives together. This is in contrast to the fact that 40% of the satisfied couples stated that they have *fun* together *and* treasure this.

A *"strong sense of self"* is cited only in the mid-range group as an important contributory factor to the longevity of their marriages (38%).

For the two variables, good *sexual relationship* (30% in all groups) and the *availability of privacy and personal space* when desired (15%), few differences emerged between the three groups. Good *joint problem solving ability* turned out to be the item ranked as the key and major factor contributing to satisfaction for all three groups. It was mentioned by 70% of both the satisfied and the mid-range couples, and by 33% of the unsatisfied pairs.

To the query on the questionnaire, "to what factors do you attribute the longevity of *your* marriage?" the satisfied couples provided the greatest number of responses:

- Satisfied–7.25 answers per person (mean)
- Mid-Range–5.12 answers per person (mean)
- Unsatisfied–3.75 answers per person (mean)

We believe this can be interpreted as a reflection of their greater awareness of what is conducive to their happiness and of an appreciation of the emotional richness of their lives. Conversely, the paucity of responses of the unsatisfied couples adequately represents their constricted relationships and overall discontent.

Discussion of the Data

Many of the findings reported above are consistent with observations, study findings and conclusions presented by other authors. Almost four decades ago Burgess and Wallin (1953) found that the presence of *good problem solving ability* bore a high positive correlation with relationship satisfaction. Nawran (1967) observed that good communication and sensitivity to the feelings of the partner characterize a happy marriage. Beavers' work (1985) highlighted the fact that successful marriages are usually *equalitarian* in power distribution. He found that a *shared value system* is also an important factor. Schwarzenauer (1980) found *shared interests* to be a major contributory element in happy marriages.

In Miller and Olsen's (1976) delineation of the circumplex model, they presented two axes of coordinates: closeness and control. The existence of both involvement↔isolation, and rigidity↔chaos characterize dysfunctional relationships. In long term satisfying relationships one sees *adaptability* rather than rigidity, *order* rather than chaos, and a *sense of attachment and belonging* rather than isolation or alienation.

In contrast to what Willi found in his work on couples in collusion (1975, 1982) alluded to earlier, in our study it appears that those who ranked as highly satisfied in their marriages had resolved whatever trauma they experienced, either prior to marriage or early in their time together, and had been able to cope with crises and transitions when they occurred in their adult years. Thus they are present and future oriented, rather than having their energy bound up in the past and allowing their history to exert a negative influence on the here and now. In addition, both seem to engage in progressive rather than regressive behaviors–apparently a hallmark of the healthy, satisfied couple.

Influence of parents' marriage. Schwarzenauer (1980) ascertained that the best chance for a harmonious marriage exists when both spouses have parents who had a good marital relationship. When individuals come from families marred by much marital discord and turbulence, or by bitter divorces, the prognosis is less than favorable. There are different ways to interpret this phenomenon. One is, as mentioned earlier, that in dysfunctional families the likelihood that children will develop personality disorders or other pathological syndromes is much higher. Emotional stability emanating from a consistently loving environment is the best precondition for and precursor of the ability to make a commitment to a long term, intimate relationship. Another explanation is that good social competence and interpersonal skills, including the willingness and capacity to be sensitive to and concerned about others, is learned in childhood. Being able to value the I, Thou, and We (Buber, 1937) in a relationship, and give them appropriate weightings in different situations is a philosophy and skill best learned from contented parents who not only nurture, guide and set limits, but serve as exemplary role models.

No specific data on the relationship between the satisfaction levels of the couples who participated and that of their parents was obtained. None of the questions were phrased specifically enough to tap into this data. This is difficult to do given that the nature of the assessment of one's parents' marriage is subjective, retrospective and has strong emotional overtones so the reliability of the responses may be dubious. Also, perceptions of what constitutes happiness change over time. Indeed, the entire question of the impact and influence of the parents' marriage on their offspring is a very complex one. Hopefully this pilot study will generate interest in other researchers to pursue further the study of the key variables in the intergenerational transmission process (Bowen, 1978). Fortunately, no one is inescapably affected by their parents. Thus those coming from unhappy, dysfunctional, "pathological" families of origin can, through life experience, through seeking other role models, and/or therapy, learn more effective ways of coping, master the unfinished issues and tasks of childhood, find healthy channels for satisfying their deficit (D) and being (B) needs (Maslow, 1970) and become able to trust sufficiently to make a commitment to an exclusive love relationship.

It is hypothesized here that some dissatisfied couples who stay together do so in an act of loyalty to their parents who they know disapprove of divorce and/or who would be profoundly distressed if they were to divorce. Unfortunately, inherent in this type of loyalty is a degree of martyrdom that can lead to enormous unhappiness and which may ultimately be converted into any number of physical or emotional maladies.

"Words of wisdom" regarding marital satisfaction. Study respondents were asked what advice they would give to others to help them achieve a satisfying relationship. Since wise "advice" can be derived as much out of positive as from negative experiences, we lumped together the responses from the three categories of subjects. In descending order of frequency, the responses were as follows:

1. Give and take, compromises   38%
2. Establish and maintain good communication   35%
3. Respect your spouse and treat him/her as an equal   28%
4. Establish a tight (close, cohesive) family   25%
5. Be supportive of your spouse   23%
6. Be sensitive to and considerate of the
   needs of your spouse   23%
7. Trust each other, be honest   23%
8. Maintain a balance between individuality
   and couplehood   23%
9. Love each other and be committed to the relationship   23%
10. Have fun together as often as possible   18%
11. Marry someone with similar values, or develop
    these together   18%
12. Share interests and activities so time together
    is well spent   18%
13. Choose a partner with a similar background.   10%
14. Choose the "right" partner   8%
15. Work together for financial security   8%

16. Be affectionate, stay in touch sensually   8%
17. Solve problems as they arise   8%
18. Be friends   8%

Fennell (1987) conducted a study of 147 couples, all in first marriages that had lasted over 20 years. He did not seem to limit the upper range of number of years married nor did he report ages and other demographic characteristics of respondents, so the two studies cannot be compared on these variables. He and his assistants located subjects through a "search and referral method" (Fennell, 1987, p. 8) that seems analogous to our networking procedure.

He also utilized Spanier's Dyadic Adjustment Scale (1976) as the main instrument for rating subjects on marital satisfaction and created a survey instrument through which couples were asked "what they believed were the characteristics they and their spouses possessed that resulted in their long term marriages" (Fennell, 1987, p. 4). Thus his study and ours were somewhat similar in methodology, in instructions to respondents, and in objective.

He found the following eight characteristics reappeared with the greatest frequency:

1. Lifetime commitment to marriage.
2. Loyalty to spouse and the expectation of reciprocity.
3. Strong, shared moral values.
4. Respect for spouse as best friend, and self disclosure to each other.
5. Commitment to sexual fidelity.
6. Desire to be a good parent.
7. Faith in God and spiritual commitment.
8. Good companion to spouse–spend a great deal of enjoyable time together over course of lifetime.

His major finding was that husbands and wives in satisfactory marriages of 20-plus years duration express high congruence regarding what they think are the important characteristics which have contributed to their long term unions. Similarly, Murstein (1980) found that in successful marriages the partners possess value consensus and role congruence. Our findings also point to a high level of concordance in each couples' assessment of the qualities and variables that make their marriages work well for them.

A comparison of the characteristics Fennell's respondents highlighted and those reported by the researchers and clinicians at the healthy family conference (Family Therapy News, 1990) show much overlap and some variation. Fennell's work emphasizes the best friend, fidelity and commitment factors more; the conference participants place much greater weight on the importance of good problem solving and coping skills. Both found that the variable of a spiritual orientation or transcendental value system seemed central; this does not emerge as quite as significant from our study population, although it was cited by some of the couples.

Our respondents, given the freedom to create their own list of essential ingredients, seem to have included all the other variables which appear on both lists, plus several more. Those additional attributes most emphasized include:

1. Being patient and understanding.
2. Listening well.
3. Doing exciting activities together, including travel–and avoiding repetition and boredom.
4. Continued sexual attraction and mutual sexual enjoyment.
5. A great deal of expressed affection.
6. Loyalty and fidelity to one another.
7. Non-interference by both sets of parents, yet closeness, to children and extended family.
8. Helping each other when requested to do so.
9. Being supportive of one another's wishes, careers and dreams.
10. Seeing spouse as being a good parent.
11. Both are trustworthy, and respect each other's integrity.
12. Like each other as people.
13. Willingness of both to compromise and take turns.

CONCLUSION

Healthy, high well-being individuals are the most apt to be attracted to a partner who is also self actualizing and has a good self image, yet is able to be considerate of, sensitive to, and capable of commitment to a significant other. Such pairings seem to produce the kind of long term marital satisfaction that was addressed in this paper.

The words of wisdom elicited from the study respondents subsume and go beyond the characteristics most often cited, and alluded to earlier, as prototypical of healthy couples and families. The concern for financial matters and sexual pleasure included in the above list are all too frequently overlooked by the experts. So, too, is the emphasis of these respondents on trust, candor, consideration and compromise.

The "essential ingredients" for long term satisfying marriages most frequently given by our study respondents were:

1. Good problem solving and coping skills;
2. Trust in each other that includes fidelity, integrity and feeling "safe";
3. Permanent commitment to the marriage;
4. Open, honest, good communication;
5. Enjoy spending time together, have fun together, good sense of humor—yet appreciate some spaces in togetherness for separate activities;
6. Shared value system, interests and activities;
7. Consideration, mutual appreciation and reciprocity—easy give and take;
8. Deep and abiding love for one another, enriched by being dear friends and lovers; continue to find one another attractive, appealing, desirable and interesting.

The cohesive family unit stressed in the literature to date does typify the satisfied couples in this sample; they have a sense of belonging to their respective families of origin and remain appropriately attached to their adult children and grandchildren. Loyalty rather than indifference or detachment to significant others is a characteristic.

It appears that these couples have intuitively and deliberately fashioned for themselves a dynamic and flexible "recipe" for a satisfying, long term marriage. Similarity and congruence of background regarding religion, education and lifestyle emerge as key factors. Endogamy rather than exogamy seems to hold part of the key to the kind of shared values that are conducive to long term pleasure and satisfaction.

The ability to live in the present and future, rather than be governed by the unhappiness or trauma and grievances of the past, seems to be one characteristic that differentiates satisfied from unsatisfied couples.

Plans are under way to replicate the present study with a less affluent, less well educated and highly professional population in the United States to see if the same factors emerge. Also, we do not know if the fact that 3/4 of the couples happened to be Jewish means the data may not be as applicable to non-Jewish couples, so in any replications a broader type of sample will be sought.

Other replications are being undertaken in Germany and perhaps Chile to see which factors appear as significant in other countries and cultures. Once all of these are completed, a variegated socioeconomic and cross-cultural comparison will be attempted to determine differences and similarities as to the essential ingredients conducive to long term marital satisfaction. Also, more attention will be given to whether there are differences in the 25-35 years of marriage group and the 35-45 year married couples, as the age span covered encompasses several stages in the life cycle and it might be useful to view these separately.

REFERENCES

Beavers, W.R. (1944). *Psychotherapy and growth: A family systems perspective.* New York: Brunner/Mazel.

Beavers, W.R. (1982). Healthy, midrange and severely dysfunctional families. In F. Walsh (Ed.), *Normal family processes,* pp. 45-66. New York: Guilford.

Beavers, W.R. (1985). *Successful marriage.* New York: Norton.

Bowen, M. (1978). *Family therapy in clinical practice.* New York: Aronson.

Bowlby, J. (1975). *Bindung. Eine Analyse der Mutter-Kind-Beziehung.* Munchen: Kindler.

Buber, M. (1937). *I and Thou.* Edinburgh: T & T Clark.

Burgess, E.W. and Wallin, P. (1953). *Engagement in marriage.* Philadelphia: Lippincott.

Family Therapy News (July/August 1990). Healthy families featured in Washington conference, p. 8.

Fennel, D.L. (1987). Characteristics of long term first marriages. Paper presented at 45th annual American Association for Marriage and Family Therapy Conference, Chicago, Illinois.

Fincham, F.D. (1991). Understanding close relationships: An attributional perspective. In S. Zelen (Ed.), *New models–New extension of attributional theory.* New York: Springer Verlag, 163-206.

Friedman, P.H. (Sept./Oct. 1987). From the foundation for well-being: The care principles of well being. *Pennsylvania Psychologist,* 10-11.

Haley, J. (1980). *Leaving home: The therapy of disturbed young people.* New York: McGraw Hill.

Jacobson, N.S. and Margolin, G. (1979). *Marital therapy: Strategies based on social learning and behavior exchange principles.* New York: Brunner/Mazel.

Kaslow, F.W. (1981). Profile of the Healthy Family. *Interaction, 4,* (1/2), 1-15, and in *The Relationship,* (1982), *8* (1), 9-24.

Kaslow, F.W. (1982). *Portrait of a Healthy Couple.* Psychiatric Clinics of North America, 5, *3,* 519-527.

Kaslow, F.W. and Schwartz, L.L. (1987). Older children of divorce: a neglected family segment. In J. Vincent (Ed.), *Advances in family intervention.* Greenwich, Conn.: Jai Press.

Lewis, J., Beavers, W.R., Gossett, J.T., and Phillips, V.A. (1976). *No single thread: Psychological health and the family system.* New York:Brunner/Mazel.

Locke, H.J. and Wallace, K.M. (1959). Short marital adjustment and prediction tests: Their reliability and validity. *Marriage and Family Living,* 21, 251-255.

Maslow, A. (1968). *Toward a psychology of being.* New York: Van Nostrand.

Maslow, A. (1970). *Motivation and personality.* New York: Van Nostrand.

Miller, B.C. and Olson, D.H.L. (1976). Clusteranalysis as a method for defining types of marriage interaction. Paper presented at National Council on Family Relations, Chicago, Illinois.

Minuchin, S. (1974). *Families and family therapy.* Cambridge, Massachusetts: Harvard University Press.

Murstein, B. (1980). Mate selection in the 1970's. *Journal of Marriage and the Family,* 42, 777-792.

Nawran, L. (1967). Communication and adjustment in marriage. *Family Process,* 6, 173-184.

Neugarten, B. (1970). Dynamics of transition of middle age to old age: Adaptations and the life cycle. *Journal of Geriatric Psychiatry,* 4, 71-87.

Olson, D.H. and Portner, J. (1983). Family adaptability and cohesion evaluation scales. In E.E. Filsinger (Ed.), *Marriage and family assessment,* pp. 299-316. Newbury Park, California: Sage.

Olson, D.H., Russell, L.S. and Sprenkle, D.H (1983). Circumplex model VI: Theoretical update. *Family Process,* 22, 69-83.

Olson, D.H., (1990). The triple threat of bridging research, theory and practice. In F.W. Kaslow (Ed.), *Voices in family psychology,* Vol. 1, pp. 361-374. Newbury Park, California: Sage.

Revenstorf, D. (1990). Eheberatung. In M. Textor (Ed.), *Helfen fur Familien,* pp. 290-311.Frankfurt: A. M. Fischer.

Sager, C.J. (1976). *Marriage contracts and couple therapy: Hidden forces in intimate relations.* New York: Brunner/Mazel.

Schwarzenauer, W. and Baur, D. (1976). Laesst sich die groessere Stress belastbarkeit von Frauen in harmonischen Ehen mit Hilfe des Ich-begriffs erklaeren? *Partnerberatung,* 13, 192-197.

Schwarzenauer, W. (1980). Was macht eine Ehe gluecklich? *Partnerberatung*, 2, 49-65.

Solomon, M.F. (1989). *Narcissism and intimacy.* New York: Norton.

Spanier, G.B. (1976). Measuring Dyadic Adjustment. New Scales for Assessing the Quality of Marriage and Similar Dyads. *Journal of Marriage and the Family,* Vol. 2, 38, 15-28.

Walsh, F. (1980). The family in later life. In Carter, E.A. and McGoldrick, M. (Eds.), *The family life cycle,* pp. 197-220. New York: Gardner Press.

Walsh, F. (1982). *Normal family processes.* New York: Guilford.

Willi, J. (1975). *Die Zweierbeziehung.* Reinbech: Towohlt. Translated (1982) as *Couples in collusion.* New York and London: Aronson.

Weitzman, L.J. (1985). *The divorce revolution: The unexpected social and economic consequences for women and children in America.* New York: Free Press.

A Poem

She did not invite anyone to the
wedding
saying it was obscene
to be hitched in public,
even though
the groom expected
hoopla
in honor of tradition and his folks.

Knowing now
that God was dead
she could hardly ask Him
to the ceremony.
Him or anybody else.

It stormed.
En route the taxi dropped a wheel
in the middle of a puddle
and the bride and groom,
waded to the curb
as horns honked
and truckers cursed at them.

Had they been ones to notice auguries
they might have cut the knot
right then and there.

Judith Morley resides at 250 Scudders Lane, Roslyn Harbor, NY 11576.
Copyright 1987 Judith Marley.

The wedding went
as planned:
No flutes and cymbals,
No special vows,
No crushed wine glass
in ancient ritual
No lifted veil
and kisses under the canopy.
No exultant families.

The miracle
is–the marriage lasted
forty years
and she always
cries at weddings.

–Judith Morley

Comprehensive Marital Therapy

Joan D. Atwood

SUMMARY. This article approaches couple therapy from several theoretical frameworks in that object relations family therapy and cognitive-behavioral marital counseling are integrated into a basic systemic orientation. The paper focuses on the three stages of couple therapy, the early, middle, and later stages, and includes a description of specific therapeutic goals relevant to each stage.

INTRODUCTION

Marital Therapy consists of an interface between three individuals, the two partners and the therapist (Kramer, 1985). The therapist has been asked to help the couple to improve some aspect of their relationship. The therapist can view their situation from several possible theoretical frameworks, some of which identify the individual as having the problem, in this case operating within an intrapsychic framework; while others view the problem as a function of a mutual exchange between two persons or as examining the resulting configuration of each member's contributing makeup, operating from some form of a system framework. The focus of this paper is primarily on a systemic orientation to marital therapy (Hoffman, 1981; Sluzki, 1978; Steinglass, 1978). However, in so doing, object relations family therapy and cognitive-behavioral marital counseling is integrated into a more systemic orientation. It is the author's contention that the

Joan D. Atwood, PhD, CSW, is Coordinator of the Graduate Programs in Marriage and Family Therapy at Hofstra University, Hempstead, NY, 11550. She is the author of *Treatment Techniques for Common Mental Disorders* and *Family Therapy: A Cognitive-Behavioral Approach*, has done extensive research and written numerous journal articles in the field of marriage and family therapy.

marital therapies are not and cannot be mutually exclusive. The marital system, comprised of two separate yet interwoven personalities joining together to create the relationship system is much too complicated to be approached by only one theoretical framework. This paper presents a discussion of the three stages of marital therapy: (1) Early Stages, (2) Middle Stages, and (3) Later Stages as approached from a more integrated perspective. Within each section, there is a description of the specific therapeutic goals relevant to that stage.

ASSUMPTIONS OF MARITAL THERAPISTS

When doing marital therapy, there are certain assumptions held by marital therapists (Napier, 1988). Some of the more major assumptions are:

1. One or both spouses in a chronically disturbed relationship will tend to misperceive the partner's motivations and personality characteristics (Meissner, 1978; Sonne & Swirsky, 1981).

2. People tend to recreate their interpersonal world by eliciting behavior from others that confirms their inner representational world and by discouraging or selectively ignoring disconfirmatory behavior (Ables & Brandsma, 1977; Willi, 1984).

3. Repetitive observation of spouse behavior that is discrepant with the schema for the perception of the spouse will result in a change in the schema (Willi, 1984).

4. Couples collude, cooperate with each other to maintain the dysfunctional symptom (Blank & Blank, 1968; Dicks, 1963; Willi, 1984).

5. The symptom serves a protective function in that it maintains the homeostasis of the system (Haley, 1965, 1973; 1976; Minuchin, 1974; Stanton, 1981).

6. Every human has a biological drive to unfold and to grow–to be the fullest s/he can be. This drive to grow may be forced underground in a person so that we cannot detect it, but we assume it is still present (Satir, 1967,1972; Whitaker, Greenberg & Greenberg, 1981).

THREE STAGES OF THERAPY

As stated above, couple therapy can be discussed in terms of the three phases of the therapeutic process: (A) Early Stages, (B) Middle Stages, and (C) Later Stages. Below is a discussion of each stage.

The Early Stages of Therapy–The Battle for Structure

There are four major therapeutic goals in the beginning stages of couple therapy. They are: (1) Resolving the Battle for Structure, (2) Joining, (3) Creating a Holding Environment, and (4) Systemic Assessment.

Resolving the Battle for Structure

From the onset, there is a Battle for Structure (Napier, 1988). The Battle for Structure determines who is in charge of therapy and under what structure the therapy will be conducted. In order for a therapist to be effective, regardless of theoretical orientation, s/he must adhere to some procedural protocol. With respect to future sessions, it is most important for the therapist to be the one who determines who will attend. If the therapist, for whatever reason, allows the contact spouse to determine which members will be present, then the therapist is allowing that client to control the therapy. In this case, the therapist has become part of the dysfunctional system and in so doing has been manipulated in much the same way as the family members.

Structuring the therapy begins when the therapist receives the inquiring spouse's phone call. The manner in which the therapist conducts him/herself on the phone, inquiries about the nature of the couple's problem, determining who will attend the first and possible future therapy sessions, how payment will be made, etc., helps the therapist to establish an appropriate working environment.

Joining

Another task to be accomplished during the first sessions is joining. Joining is the process by which an empathic rapport is developed with the clients (Minuchin, 1974). Effective therapy depends mainly on the ability of the therapist to comprehend how each spouse is experiencing the marital problem and what it is that each desires from the marriage. The therapist's reflections serve as an empathic connection with the clients, through which each can feel understood, appreciated and safe. It is through this sensitive and delicate thread that therapist earns each spouse's trust. The deeper the joining, the deeper the trust. This trusting environment creates the ability of the part of the clients to risk changes.

Creating a Holding Environment

Creating an environment conducive to change is the third task to be accomplished in the beginning stages of couple therapy. This is called creating a "holding environment" (Winnicott, 1965) in which both spouses can co-exist, tolerate the others' presence and involvement, while the therapist acts as both support and defense system. Each spouse is then free to consider his/her position and approach, without fear of intrusion from the other spouse. The holding environment also affords each spouse a safe environment in which to re-explore the other, the relationship, and more importantly, him/herself. This is accomplished through each observing the therapist joining with and "being there" for the other spouse, but not at the expense of the other. Each spouse realizes that they can share each other with the therapist without fearing disloyalty, bias, or threat. In this way, each spouse learns that s/he can once again be open, able to share and express him/herself to the other. Once this facet of therapy has begun, an assessment of the marital difficulties and each spouse's contribution to the failed solutions, can then be examined.

Systemic Assessment

Systems theory, as presented here, requires the therapist to obtain as complete as possible an understanding of how and why two individuals are interacting as they do. In order to do this, it is useful to obtain information about the present marital situation on two separate levels: the historical and the present. These two levels of analysis are examined within the context of (1) the couple's family structure, (2) the couple's relational history, and (3) the couple's relational process.

The Present Marital Situation. Marital situations can be divided into three experiential levels: the extended family, the spousal relationship, and the personality of each individual. During this phase, the therapist examines the past and present relationships of each spouse in order to better understand how each spouse typically functions within relationships. In general, based on early parent-child interactions and ongoing socialization, individuals develop a preferred way of relating to others. This then becomes the perceptual set as to how they view others and how they expect others to view them. In many ways, perceptual sets determine predictable ways of interacting with others, roles in life, and what individuals expect out of life or from others. In other words, as Watzlawick, Beavin, and Jackson (1967) point out, we create our own reality or more colloquially stated, "We get what we ask for" (Watzlawick, Weakland, & Fisch, 1974). An examination of each spouse's three experiential levels helps the therapist define these perceptual role sets, as well as when and how they developed.

Gathering information about the couple's family structure. Beginning with an examination of extended family, each spouse is asked to examine his/her parental relationships, the parent's marriage, his/her siblings, and any other significant relationships. Specific interactional patterns, roles, structure, boundaries, familial or traditional beliefs/ values are identified for the purpose of understanding how these familial attributes are influencing the meaning of a spouse's behavior or the meaning s/he attaches to the other's behavior (Aponte & Von Deuser, 1981; Kantor & Lehr, 1975; Kantor & Kuperman, 1985; Minuchin, 1974; Stanton, 1980). This information can be very easily gathered using a genogram (Francis, 1988; Marlin, 1989; McGoldrick & Gerson, 1985). In addition, patterns of relating such as proximity/distance and enmeshment/disengagement are examined (Minuchin, 1974).

If the couple is experiencing more severe marital problems related to unresolved historical issues stemming from the family of origin, more time needs to be spent on these issues. In these cases, it is wise for the therapist to use a more psychodynamic approach (Bowen, 1978; Scharff, 1989; Slipp, 1988).

Next, the marital relationship is explored. In this case, each spouse is asked to identify the couple's positive and negative qualities, strengths and weaknesses, and division of labor (Jacobson, 1978; Stuart, 1980). In this way, the therapist obtains an understanding of how the couple makes decisions, solves problems, negotiates and resolves conflicts and how each spouse asserts him/herself.

Finally, the intrapersonal level is explored. Here each spouse explores his/her own personal beliefs, values, strengths and weaknesses in order to help the therapist gain a basic understanding of each spouse's psychological sense of self, emotionality, relational sensitivities, and adaptability.

Gathering information around the couple's relational history. Within this contextual framework, the therapist examines each spouse's transcending relational history (Ackerman, 1958; Bowen, 1966, 1971, 1978; Kerr, 1981; Spark, 1974, 1981). Here, there is an examination of each individual's development, the passage through his/her life cycle events and a review of his/her family of origin patterns and issues. The therapist needs to obtain as comprehensive as possible a picture of each spouse's physiological, cognitive, emotional, and social development. The therapist is particularly concerned with whether each spouse moved through his/her developmental milestones as expected or if some form of developmental abnormality (speech delayed); deviation (repeating a grade); disruption or an unstable environmental condition (moving around a lot during grade school years); or a trauma (unexpected death of a family member) adversely affected some area of his/her development.

With regard to life cycle events passage (McGoldrick & Carter, 1982), the therapist is concerned with whether or not each spouse successfully achieved certain developmental tasks. For example, most young adults are expected to have matured to the point of wanting to leave home, becoming self sufficient through work, and developing social relationships. If they did successfully pass through a transitional stage, the therapist wants to know: How did they achieve it? If they did not, was it due to premature or delayed arrival of this stage? What family factors were operating at the time? The basic question here is that if there was a problem, why was this phase of interpersonal development a problem? From this information, the therapist can then better understand how developmentally mature and ready each spouse is, and to what extent each spouse is able to effectively manage and cope with interpersonal issues (Haley, 1973; Stanton, 1978; Weakland, Fisch, Watzlawick & Bodin, 1974).

With regard to transgenerational patterns, the therapist is interested in having each spouse become more knowledgeable about his/her own family history as well as that of the other spouse (Feldman, 1976). Transgenerational patterns are identifiable through the study of family traditions and rituals and the symbolic preferred ways of relating. These transgenerational patterns are conveyed and maintained through the ascription of certain meaning to particular types of behavior, interactions, or events. These transgenerational patterns provide each family member with some sense of rootedness, family and personal identity. The therapist is particularly interested in learning how each spouse upholds his/her familial beliefs and practices (regarding gender roles; division of labor; use of violence, illness or money; the meaning given to certain behaviors or events and the customary ways of coping with them) within the present marriage (Spark, 1981). In this manner, the therapist is better able to understand why each spouse chooses to interact with the other in a particular manner, over particular items, at particular times, etc. This information also enables the therapist to understand why one spouse's response is not always appreciated by the other; or, why one may not be able to respond as the other would like. In this way, the therapist is better able to understand the type of "dance" that the spouses are involved in, whether they are dancing the same or different steps, and whether those steps are appropriate or inappropriate to the music.

Gathering information about the couple's relational process. As stated above, the therapist acquires the above contextual framework in order to formulate a hypothesis, determine therapeutic goals, and develop a treatment plan. This is accomplished through a comprehensive assessment process. Here, the therapist begins this assessment process by appreciating the presenting problem or the clients' reason for being in therapy on both an explicit and implicit level (Sager, 1976). On the explicit level, the therapist can examine the problem in context. For example, s/he can use "tracking" to establish the interactional sequence of events. Here the therapist assumes that the symptom is a homeostatic mechanism regulating marital transactions (Haley, 1973; Jackson, 1965). At this point, the therapist has moved to a more strategic level of analysis and the goal here is to change the dysfunctional sequence of behaviors as shown by the marital couple appearing for treatment (Haley, 1973; Stanton, 1981). On the explicit level, the couple's problem identifies the problem area in need of a solution which they have been unable to achieve.

On an implicit level, the problem represents an interactional pattern or dance, a dance that even though it is destructive is functioning in a protective way to maintain the present system. Thus, the dance is seen as having purpose for both spouses, collectively and separately. It has a different symbolic significance for each spouse, which cannot be ignored, but which disturbs the other spouse and threatens the existence of the relationship. Ironically, the symbolic meaning of the presenting problem often is the very thing which first drew the spouses together but which now irritates and divides them. Thus, in many ways, the seeds for the destruction of the relationship are present from the very beginning of the relationship. For example, one spouse may have positively defined the other's outspokenness. In many ways, what was the original attraction to the other represents an attempt to rectify some past family of origin relational/personal issue. This issue then can become an unconscious process within the present marital relationship. So, that inevitably, what once was positively defined as outspokeness may eventually be redefined as bullying. This occurs because emotional reactivity is reawakened within each spouse. The outspokenness now makes the individual feel incompetent, something that perhaps was originally elicited by a stern father in the family of origin. These feelings of incompetency may cause the individual to behave in incompetent ways, causing the other spouse to increase his/her outspokenness, believing that this is what is needed since it was successful in the past. In turn, this causes the other to respond by escalating his/her own position. This reciprocating escalation and entrenchment represents a reenactment of historically unresolved issues. Each spouse's own pre-relational emotional issues have become reactivated. The marital partners become more and more polarized around these issues with each sphere of potentialities or possibilities becoming more and more narrow.

Diagnostically, when the therapist views the presenting problem, the observed and related interactional pattern in this way, s/he obtains a basis for formulating a hypothesis as to what (often unconscious) meaning the couple's interaction has for them. This affords each spouse a greater understanding of his/her own and other's behavior, as well as an understanding of the reasons for the problem. This observation can provide each spouse with some sense of relief and increases his/her tolerance for the other's undesirable behavior as well as for their combined struggle.

Information about the spouses' family and marital relationships and about each one's intrapsychic dynamics may be directly acquired through such diagnostic techniques as: genograms, sculpting, circular questioning, life cycle stages assessment, and gleaned during the first therapeutic sessions in order to assess each spouse's: (1) receptivity to therapeutic directives, (2) desire for change, (3) motivation, (4) reasons for entering therapy at this time, (5) attempted solutions, (6) ability to accept and profit from change, and (7) ability to be introspective. Some of the following specific questions will help the therapist assess these areas. Questions 1 and 2 will help the therapist determine what internal and external pressures have caused the couple to come into therapy at this time. Question 3 identifies what has been tried to remedy this situation. Questions 4, 5, and 6 assess a spouse's ability to recognize and accept desirable change.

1. Why are you entering therapy at this particular time?
2. What is happening in your lives at this time (contextual issues)?
3. What have you tried to do to resolve this problem?
4. What is it that you want to get out of therapy?
5. What is the smallest amount of change that would constitute success for you?
6. How would you (your relationship) be different if the problem were resolved?

In order to assess each spouse's motivation for change and responsiveness to therapeutic directives, the behavioral phase of therapy begins. Cognitive-behavioral techniques are used to examine secondary gain around the presenting problem, to determine therapeutic goals, to set up the therapeutic contract, and to accomplish cognitive restructuring wherever needed (Beck, 1976). Here the therapist can also assess the anxiety level around change as measured by the willingness of each to carry out specific tasks assigned by the therapist, such as a homework assignment. The spouses' levels of anxiety will indicate two things to the therapist:

1. Its presence or absence within either spouse will serve as an indicator of the prognosis of the case. Just as "necessity is the mother of invention," anxiety can elicit change in marriages.

2. The more anxious spouse is the more motivated spouse. This indicates to the therapist which one to engage first and from whom to expect the greatest initial movement.

The homework assignments are generally behavioral and can be some form of "caredays" (Epstein & Williams, 1981; Jacobson, 1978; Knox, 1971; Lieberman, Levine, Wheeler, Sanders, & Wallace, 1976; Stuart, 1976, 1980). The couple is instructed to spend at least one or two days a week doing premarital activities, the activities that they recognize as the "good times" they once experienced during their dating period. This directive is given to determine how bankrupted their marital account is. If it still has any equity, then faithful deposits by each of them is required. No withdrawals are permitted. In other words, difficult times are to be kept to a minimum and under stringent control to prevent any further erosion of their relationship or self-esteem.

The spouses' responsiveness to therapeutic directives can be assessed through an initial homework assignment which involves both of them, and which they each have helped to design. Responsiveness is assessed by how far each went with performing the assignment. This exercise provides the therapist with additional diagnostic information, such as:

1. Whether the couple or either spouse is still capable of enjoying courting behavior. The question is whether their bank account (relationship) is bankrupted or whether deposits can still be made by either spouse in order to keep the account open. This will also help the therapist determine how motivated each is toward staying married and establishing a positive foundation upon which therapy can occur.

2. How hurt and resistant each spouse is, is determined by observing how they respond to each other.

3. Understanding how expansive the problem is in terms of the entire relationship.

After a systemic assessment has begun, the therapist can then share with the couple his/her understanding of the marital problem and what s/he believes should be the therapeutic task. It is important to note that the therapeutic interpretation need not be "truth." However, it does need to be relevant–believable by the couple. The therapist can formulate the hypothesis by positively reframing the problem so as to instill hope and stimulate positive motivation and relationship enhancing behavior. In this manner also, the couple is given a new perception of the reality of their relationship. They are able to "see" their problem in a new way–a way they have not considered in the past. It is this new perception of the couple's reality which provides for the potential of change.

For example, from the current assessment data, the therapist could state that a couple's problem is due to each spouse attempting to have things his/her own way. The therapist positively reframes/relabels the problem as being a problem of family loyalties (Boszormenyi-Nagy, 1973): each spouse is battling with the other in the hopes of proving his/her family as "victor." The therapist, having information about the couple's families of origin can then present historical information as to why this is the case. This hypothesis is presented in order to bring about some immediate relief to the marital system and permit the spouses to re-address their respective positions. The impact of the reframe upon the couple is to get each to rethink his/her position with the other and to help them "see" their struggle in a new light. As long as the presented hypothesis is isomorphic with the couple's struggle, it will provide them with new possibilities for change. The couple's reaction to the reframe further provides the therapist with feedback as to whether (1) s/he has sufficiently joined with each spouse, (2) s/he has accurately assessed their problem and, (3) each spouse is ready to engage in the therapeutic process. If the therapist has accomplished this, then s/he can safely continue the assessment of the problem while continuing to make therapeutic interventions. If not, then the therapist needs to continue to develop rapport with each spouse until a positively reframed hypothesis proves viable. This phase of couple therapy is often referred to as hypothesis testing and reduction. Once the couple and the therapist have agreed on the nature of the problem, then the therapist and couple need to devise a workable and acceptable contractual therapeutic relationship.

During problem identification and therapeutic goal determination, the therapist has gained additional experience in working with each spouse. This direct relational experience provides the therapist with assessment data to test each spouse's flexibility or motivation to alter his/her position and approach to the other.

Middle Stages of Therapy–The Battle for Initiative

Resolving the Battle for Initiative

The Battle for Initiative (Napier & Whitaker, 1978) revolves around the determination of whose therapy it is, who is in charge of the therapy, and how much each spouse is motivated for change. The process is begun by the therapist inviting each spouse to explore his/her perception of the current relationship, and whether this situation is similar to previous ones. If either spouse does not respond to the therapist's invitation, then the therapist does nothing more until the non-responsive spouse finds meaning and commits him/herself to their problem and therapy. With spouses who respond, but whose commitment is hindered by their need to maintain control over their emotions or the situation, the therapist might try to help them become emotionally involved by making a reflective and observational statement, such as, "Why don't you stop pretending that it doesn't hurt to feel ignored and just experience your own unhappiness."

The Therapist's Two Functions During This Phase

Keep Focused. The therapist's first function during the middle stages is to keep the spouses squarely on target, while facilitating them to risk vulnerability, to explore themselves, and to act in their best interests, without accepting responsibility for or investing in the outcome. If the therapist attempts to persuade or lead a client, then s/he can be held responsible for the directive's outcome. The therapist has then assumed the spouse's responsibility and is determining how the spouse should act and what the spouse needs. As Whitaker (1978) states, the therapist cannot adopt his/her clients; s/he can only provide them with foster care: that is, the therapist can provide the couple with a safe, nurturing environment, having some limits, and offer them the opportunity to share and explore issues. However, the drive and responsibility for change remains with the spouses. The clients decide on the goals of therapy. The therapist and the clients explore ways of reaching the goals. The clients' decide whether or not they are willing to extend themselves. If they are, then it is their responsibility to accomplish the goals.

Use Yourself. The second function of the therapist during the middle phases of couple therapy is the therapist's use of self (Real, 1990). Here, the therapist monitors him/herself in terms of visceral and mental reactions to the couple for two reasons. The first reason is that the use of self can be used to read the anxiety level of each spouse. Low anxiety levels often are identified as little motivation for change. This could mean that the therapist is working too hard and has in the process lowered the client's anxiety. At the other extreme, overly high anxiety levels can indicate that the couple is functioning in an environment that is above safe limits. In this case, it is possible that they have lost their ability to cope effectively. In the first case, the therapist needs to sit back, relax, and allow the tension to build up uncomfortably within the couple. Otherwise, the couple may not ever take responsibility for their therapy. In the second case, the therapist needs to actively intervene by either interrupting the flow of discourse or discussing irrelevant items in order to bring the anxiety level of the couple down.

The second use of self requires the therapist to share his/her emotional or mental reactions to the couple, to the extent s/he is comfortable. The therapist's gut reactions or associations to the material, when shared, provide the spouses with metaphorical signals that often are useful in getting through verbalizations, intellectualizations, and other emotional defenses. These sometimes have the impact of a hot knife cutting through butter, speaking straight to the heart of the matter. An example would be, "Does he always react to you in this rational way when you speak to him emotionally?" The therapist's shared reactions act as a symbolic representation, allowing him/her to get through the emotionality of the one and overintellectualization of the other, providing the first with insight and the second with emotional stimulation.

The Two Stage Process

The process of therapy occurring during the middle phase involves accomplishing two therapeutic tasks. The first stage is what Whitaker

(1978) calls the Individual-Regressive Stage and the second stage is called the Emotional Deactivation stage.

The Individual-Regressive Stage. There are two prerequisites to the individual-regressive stage: (1) a rapprochement and (2) a meta-medium.

Rapprochement. Rapprochement refers to the forming of a harmonious alliance between the therapist and each spouse. Its importance here is to have both spouses actively involved in their couple therapy. It is critically important for the therapist to recognize motivational differences between the two spouses and manage them accordingly. Specifically, one spouse is usually more anxious than the other. This tends to be the identified patient or the symptomatic spouse. Generally, this is the person who is most desirous of change. This spouse requires some immediate relief and assurance. Also, the therapist needs to join with this spouse first so that s/he feels understood. Failure to achieve this will bring couple therapy to a quick close, since this spouse will find him/herself overwhelmed with anxiety or pain which is beyond his/her ability to manage. This can cause this spouse to become hopelessly resigned to giving up. Once the therapist has joined with this spouse, s/he can then carefully join with the other spouse. This must be a careful connection because this spouse typically sees him/herself as not contributing to the problem. This second spouse tends to believe it is the partner's problem and sees him/herself as over functioning. This spouse needs to have an extremely strong relationship with the therapist. If not, then when the therapist attempts to probe his/her contribution to the problem, especially involving emotional issues, this spouse will balk and could prematurely end the therapy. Bowen (1978) and Fogarty (1976) have described the less anxious spouse's position as that of the intellectualizer and distancer, and the more anxious spouse as that of enmeshed one and pursuer. The more the first spouse or therapist attempts to heat up the session with emotional issues, the more the second spouse will attempt to seek a rational or logical way of dealing with these issues. If these rational efforts fail, s/he will tend to fall silent and ultimately withdraw.

Once the therapist has achieved a strong and viable relationship with the over-intellectualized spouse, the therapist then needs to debunk the concept of the symptomatic spouse in his/her mind. Each spouse needs to understand and acknowledge his/her contributions to the problem, that they both are cooperating with each other in some way to maintain the problem. Otherwise the therapy is doomed to fail. If the clients do not accept equal responsibility for the problem, therapy then will serve to validate and sustain the dysfunctional behavior on both parts. Through the continued efforts of the therapist, a deeper trusting relationship is developed, which permits self-exploration of emotionally laden issues on a personal and individual basis. The therapist takes every opportunity to encourage, validate, coach, and protect such self exploration from interference or intrusion from the other spouse.

Creating the meta-medium. Much of the resistance from either spouse to the development of rapprochement and to self exploration, particularly with the over intellectualized spouse, can be overcome through the use of a meta-medium: a symbolic representational state, that is, using metaphors, analogies, stories, or imagery to convey a right brain, non-verbal, fully identifiable, experiential and comprehensible message. The symbolic image has the power of directly arousing us and being experienced by us, since it does not require pattern recognition, discrimination, decoding and assignment of meaning as does verbally learned language processing, which is primarily controlled by the left brain. Right brain communication enables a therapist to go beyond a spouse's intellectualized or verbalized defenses by communicating through a non-verbal medium. It has the ability of cutting to the core of a matter since it triggers off images that convey strong and powerful emotional meaning, either from memory or conjured up. The meta-medium can also be used as a viaduct for conveying unarticulated emotional experiences to others. The therapist or the spouse may be struck by some word, mannerism, or tone during the session, as someone else is describing or relating a point. It stirs within the one spouse a mental or emotional response. This sensually stimulated experience cannot be adequately or fully verbalized. It causes a symbolic representation to emerge within that person which can be conveyed to others through a metaphor or an image. This permits spouses and the therapist effectively and gently to communicate with each other, without getting caught in lexical trappings or blocked by intellectual defenses. In this way, each of the spouses is able to begin the individual regression process of delving deeply into him/herself in order to: (1) explore how s/he contributes to the marital problem, and (2) identify where these behavioral dynamics stem from and why they are not functioning as one would wish them to. Through this process, each spouse becomes more in touch with his/her own feelings, perceptions, and thoughts, and their meanings. As each spouse regresses within his/her own personal depths and past relationship history, s/he is capable of working through such emotional and relational difficulties, emerging more whole as a person and better able to manage relationships.

Another strategy used to break through resistance is the use of the paradox. Since Haley (1976) believes that dysfunctional interaction patterns are utilized to maintain homeostasis in the marital system, they are therefore functional for the couple in that they maintain the balance (even if the couple is seriously concerned about them). In other words, he feels that the dysfunctionality is functional in that it preserves the status quo. By using the paradox, Haley hopes to force couples to abandon their dysfunctional behavior by engaging in a power struggle with the therapist. In paradoxical interventions, the couple is in effect directed to "disobey" the therapist. Should they follow the therapist's instructions and continue the prescribed behavior, they are obeying the therapist, and therefore, give the therapist more power. The therapist has gained control by making the symptom appear at his/her direction. If they refuse to obey the paradoxical instruction, they move toward improvement. Thus, the couple told not to change often defies the therapist's directive: the partners begin to change to prove the therapist wrong in assuming that they could not change.

Emotional Deactivation. Once the therapist has established both the rapprochement and the meta-medium, then the emotional deactivation process can begin. This is what Winnicott (1965) defined as a therapeutic holding environment, which allows each spouse, in turn, to explore his/her own emotional concerns while the other remains emotionally unreactive. The more anxious spouse generally begins the individual regression process, while the non-symptom bearing spouse attempts to remain non-reactive and tolerant of what s/he hears the other saying or feeling. In the beginning the therapist must often intervene to help the listening spouse remain still and to encourage the speaking spouse to continue despite the other's undesirable responses to the one's personal disclosure. This process is continued until the therapist believes it is time for the spouses to reverse roles. The increased ability of one spouse to explore and give expression to inner feelings and thoughts without feeling threatened by the other interrupting helps to build his/her ability to act in his/her own best interests, become desensitized to self expression, and to allow him/herself to be emotionally vulnerable. The listening spouse builds up his/her tolerance to hear and experience unpleasant verbal and emotional statements, without feeling the need to respond to such statements.

However, the first time the other spouse attempts it, this second individuation may prove threatening to both spouses, since the therapist is temporarily switching his alliance. The first spouse may be concerned with loss of her intermediary. The second, more resistant spouse may now be concerned with having to dare to become emotionally vulnerable; s/he also may question how certain s/he is about the therapist being a good intermediary, especially after siding with the other first. This is a tricky transition which depends greatly on the therapist's ability to join–to be experienced as genuine and non-partial. With the first go around with the second spouse, the therapist needs to be quite direct and strongly push this spouse in order to help this spouse get past his/her self-denial. What makes the problem more difficult is that the intellectualizing spouse often views this intellectualizing as a strength. In essence, the therapist is threatening to turn his/her world topsy-turvy, leaving him/her weak and defenseless. If a strong enough rapprochement has been established with him/her, then the therapist can encourage him/her to begin his/her own individual-regression, publicly. If not, then the therapist either has to develop this rapprochement further, or, if the one spouse appears totally resistant to any attempt to either enter rapprochement or try what the therapist is suggesting, then the therapist needs to strongly challenge this spouse as to how they (couple) expect their problem to be resolved, if this spouse refuses to help. This stance is to be strongly held so that pressure and anxiety are built up, not only within this particular spouse, but also in the other, whose built-up anxiety spills over into his/hers. The tension of the lack of movement within the session helps him or her overcome such resistance. Once this spouse has begun the process, then the focus can be alternated between the spouses, repeatedly for the purpose of systematically desensitizing each spouse and deactivating the emotional reactivity. Spouses are once again able to experience each other and themselves more fully, without threat of judgement or verbal attacks.

After this process of alternating individual-regression has effectively begun, increased individual-differentiation has occurred. Each spouse has become either de-enmeshed with the other or reunited with his/her emotional field. Each has regained a truer sense of self. They not only are in touch with who they are, what makes tick and why, but they are also now at a point how they can walk a different road than formerly taken–a road that can offer them a more desirable sense of self–a road that can help them remain free and vulnerable without fear–that can help them become more effective in bonding and management of interpersonal relationships; that can improve their ability to emotionally express themselves and communicate more effectively with each other. The therapeutic alliance between the spouses and the therapist can now proceed to the next and final stage of therapy.

Later Stages of Therapy–The Battle for Closure

In the final stages of therapy, uncovered information about each spouse's behavioral dynamics, gathered through his/her own individual-regression, is used as a stepping off platform for: (1) personal development, (2) marital enhancement, (3) bonding, (4) effective communication, and (5) closure.

Personal Development

If it becomes apparent that either spouse is dissatisfied with what s/he found through his/her individual-regression exploration, then the therapist can offer him/her Whitaker's (1978) Language of Options. The therapist offers each spouse the opportunity to re-empower him/herself, in terms of self-determination and responsibility. For each spouse, it remains a matter of choice. Each spouse is stimulated and encouraged to think about what s/he wishes to do with his/her newly gained state of being. Specifically, the therapist proposes two thoughts for each spouse to ponder. The first is designed to free up each spouse, so as to renew his/her belief that nothing is written in stone. The therapist encourages the client not only to rethink his/her emotional state but also to imagine how s/he would like it to be. So, the therapist indicates to each spouse, "It doesn't have to be like that. You don't have to see things that way anymore." Next, the therapist encourages him/her to mobilize his/her inner forces, with the support of the other spouse and therapist. The other spouse will usually be supportive once s/he senses that s/he will need similar support form his/her spouse as well, if s/he expects to be able to make similar changes. The therapist primes a spouse's self-determination by asking the question, "Well, what do you want to do about it?"

Marital Enhancement

At this point in therapy, the appreciation of each other's separate histories now becomes the main focus. Marital Enhancement can be developed. The behavioral contingency of reciprocity can be used to increase positive marital interactions. Reciprocity involves the mutual exchange of positive reinforcers in a way which the partners see as equitable over time (Azrin, Naster, & Jones, 1973; Patterson & Hops, 1972; Weiss et al, 1973). At this point, they have learned a lot about one another through each listening to the other's individual-regressive process. They have learned that they may speak with similar words and mannerisms, which have quite often different meanings attached to them. They have further learned that such differences in his/her language have been derived through familial contexts and personal experiential worlds foreign to the other. Each spouse has now learned what the other's language means, the duality of meaning that specific events, gestures, words have for both of them. This new knowledge can have significant impact upon their marriage, with the potential of enhancing their relationship and making their communication more meaningful and effective. They are now able to understand and be understood, validate and acknowledge one another, and communicate in ways that each has learned is more meaningful to the other. Equally important, they are better able to negotiate and manage disagreements, since they have gained new insight as to what it means to the other when one of them acts in a certain way, or why certain issues have greater or lesser importance for each other and where these sensitivities originated. They have gone through what Napier (1988) refers to as a "reparenting experience."

Bonding

This enhanced bonding will help to maintain them through the difficult times in their marriage. It has been acquired through three experiential processes. The first has been ongoing, from the onset of therapy, often expressed through "care days." These care days have helped to sustain the relationship throughout the therapy while the therapist has helped each spouse begin to differentiate through the individual-regression process. The second process is the cogent experience of the differentiation and individual-regression process that they have witnessed and shared together.

Effective Communication

Effective communication is based on mutual understanding and respect of each other's experiential history and personal struggles with that history. Here the couple is taught six behavioral guidelines to effective communication as outlined by Gurman (1977). They are: (1) reports of perceptions and judgements should be acknowledged to be subjective; (2) specific feelings in contrast to ideas associated with an issue should be expressed directly; (3) the expresser should include an acknowledgement of the positive side to the issue; (4) descriptions of thoughts, feelings, and perceptions of events should be specific; (5) the interpersonal message of what specific constructive action the expresser would like from the listener should be stated explicitly; and (6) a message concerning the expresser's feelings or personal request also should convey empathy for the listener's position. Each can be a more effective helpmate and be experienced as that by the other. This mutual experience becomes a reciprocal enhancing movement for the marriage. As this bonding and reciprocating and enhancing experience becomes the mainstay of the therapeutic process, the therapist gradually retires into the background while this part of therapy is actively conducted by the spouses. The therapist's role has narrowed to (1) a reassuring presence to come to their aid when the process breaks down, (2) to advise either spouse as to how to better manage a particular phase of interaction, when asked or (3) to coach them, reminding them of things they do and don't do and why.

Closure

After this reciprocating and enhancing experience has become a more or less practiced way of dealing with each other, couples tend to pull back from treatment. At this time, the therapist may inform them that some core issues may remain for each and may resurface at some point in the marriage. If they wish, they may elect to work on these issues now or they may wish to return to therapy later when these issues resurface. In any event, because these core issues are concerned with each spouse's extended family, each spouse is encouraged to continue his/her individual work within his/her family of origin. If the couple decide to continue in therapy, then family of origin members may be asked to join them in the therapy sessions so that this focus can be more directly explored and worked. In this work, the therapist acts as consultant, since the couple have learned to handle many issues on their own.

CONCLUSIONS

It was the purpose of this paper to present a more integrated approach to marital therapy. In so doing, we presented a basic systemic framework and integrated into it object relations family therapy and cognitive-behavioral marriage counseling. We acknowledge that to accomplish this integration is no easy task and certainly one article is not going to give coverage to the voluminous amount of work already published in the field. However, it is a beginning, from which we can present three general rules.

General Rule I

Initially, use the structural approach to enter the couple structure–joining, accommodating, testing boundaries, restructuring, unbalancing, increasing intensity etc. Use a strategic approach to enter the couple process–symptom function and maintenance, communication rules which define the couple relationship, paradox for breaking resistance, cycle of interaction, etc.

General Rule II

If the couple is experiencing severe marital discord stemming from unresolved themes in their family of origin, through the use of a genogram, use a more object-relations (psychodynamic) approach to exploring these historical patterns as they relate to present functioning.

General Rule III

Use cognitive-behavioral interventions in the initial stages of therapy to assess motivation to change by giving assignments such as caring days, and to set up the initial therapeutic contract. During the middle stages of therapy, use behavioral communication skill-building to facilitate couple communication and cognitive restructuring to help facilitate more positive thinking. Use reciprocity and relationship enhancement skills to increase bonding in the later stages of therapy.

REFERENCES

Ables, B. & Brandsma, J. (1977). *Therapy for couples.* San Francisco, CA: Jossey-Bass.

Ackerman, N. (1958). *The psychodynamics of family life.* New York: Basic Books.

Aponte, H. & Von Deuser, J. (1981). Structural family therapy. In A. Gurman & P. Kniskern (Eds.) *Handbook of family therapy.* New York: Brunner/Mazel.

Azrin, N., Naster, B., & Jones, E. (1973). Reciprocity counseling: A rapid learning-based procedure for marital counseling. *Behavioral Research and Therapy,* 11,365-382.

Beck, A. (1976). *Cognitive therapy and emotional disorders.* New York: International Universities Press.

Beck, D. (1975). Research findings on the outcomes of marital counseling. *Social Casework,* 56,153-181.

Blank, R. & Blank, G. (1968). *Marriage and personal development.* New York: Columbia University Press.

Boszormenyi-Nagy, I. & Spark, G. (1973). *Invisible loyalties.* New York: Harper & Row.

Bowen, M. (1966). The use of family theory in clinical practice. *Comprehensive Psychiatry,* 7, 345-374.

Bowen, M. (1971). Family therapy and group therapy. In H. Kaplan & B. Sadock (Eds.) *Comprehensive group psychiatry.* Baltimore: Williams and Wilkins.

Bowen, M. (1978). *Family therapy in clinical practice.* New York: Jason Aronson.

Dicks, H. (1963). *Marital tensions.* New York: Basic Books.

Epstein, N. & Williams, A. (1981). Behavioral approaches to the treatment of marital discord. In G. Sholevar. (Ed.), *The handbook of marriage and marital therapy.* New York: SP Medical and Scientific Books.

Feldman, L. (1976). Depression and marital interaction. *Family Process,* 15, 389-395.

Fogarty, T. (1976). Marital crisis. In P. Guerin (Ed.), *Family therapy theory and practice.* New York: Gardener Press.

Francis, M. (1988). The skeleton in the cupboard: Experiential genogram work for family therapy trainees. *Journal of Family Therapy.* 10(2), 135-152.

Gurman, A. (1977). Much vigor, little rigor. *Contemporary Psychology,* 22, 67-68.

Haley, J. (1965). *Strategies of psychotherapy.* New York: Grune & Stratton.

Haley, J. (1973). *Uncommon therapy: The psychiatric techniques of Milton H. Erikson,* M.D. New York: Norton.

Haley, J. (1976). *Problem solving therapy.* San Francisco: Jossey Bass.

Hoffman, L. (1981). *Foundations of family therapy.* New York: Brunner/Mazel.

Jacobson, N. (1978). Contingency contracting with couples: Redundancy and caution. *Behavioral Therapy,* 9, 679.

Jackson, D..(1965). Family rules: The marital quid pro quo. *Archives of General Psychiatry,* 12, 589-594.

Kantor, D. & Lehr, W. (1975). *Inside the family.* San Francisco: Jossey Bass.

Kantor, D. & Kuperman, W. (1985). The clients interview of the therapist. *Journal of Marital and Family Therapy,* 11,225-244.

Kerr, M. (1981). Family systems theory and therapy. In A. Gurman & P. Kniskern (Eds.) *Handbook of family therapy.* New York: Brunner/Mazel.

Knox, D. (1971). *Marriage happiness: A behavioral approach to counseling.* Champaign: Research Press.

Kramer, J. (1985). *Family interfaces.* New York: Brunner/Mazel.

Lieberman, R., Levine, J., Wheeler, E., Sanders, N., Wallace, C. (1976). Experimental evaluation of marital group therapy. Behavioral: interaction-insight formats. *Acta Scandinavica,* Supplement.

Marlin E. (1989). *Genograms.* Chicago: Contemporary Books.

McGoldrick, M. & Carter, E. (1982). The family life cycle. In F. Walsh (Ed.), *Normal Family Processes.* New York: Guilford.

McGoldrick, M. & Gerson R. (1985). *Genograms in Family Assessment.* New York: Norton.

Meissner, W. (1978). The conceptualization of marriage and marital disorders from a psychoanalytic perspective. In T. Paolino & B. McGrady (Eds.), *Marriage and marital therapy: Psychoanalytic, behavioral, and system theory perspectives.*

Minuchin, S. (1974). *Families and family therapy.* Cambridge, Mass.: Harvard University Press.

Napier, G. & Whitaker, C. (1978). *The family crucible.* New York: Harper & Row.

Napier, A. (1988). *The fragile bond.* New York: Harper & Row Publishers.

Patterson, G. & Hops, H. (1972). Coersion, a game for two: Intervention techniques for marital conflict. In R. Ulrich & P. Mountjoy (Eds.), *The experimental analysis of social behavior.* New York: Appleton-Century-Crofts.

Real, T. (1990). The therapeutic use of self in constructionist systemic therapy. *Family Process,* 29, (3), pp. 255-272.

Sager, C. J. (1976). *Marriage contracts and couples therapy.* New York: Brunner/ Mazel.

Satir, V. (1967). *Conjoint family therapy.* Palo Alto, California: Science and Behavior Books.

Satir, V. (1972). *Peoplemaking.* Palo Alto, California: Science and Behavior Books.

Scharff, J. (1989). *Foundations of object relations family therapy.* New York: Jason Aronson.

Slipp, S. (1988). *The technique and practice of object relations family therapy.* New York: Jason Aronson.

Sluzki, C. (1978). Marital therapy from a systems therapy perspective. In T. Paolino & B. McGrady (Eds.), *Marriage and marital therapy.* New York: Brunner/Mazel.

Sonne, J. & Swirsky, D. (1981). Self-object considerations in marriage and marital therapy. In P. Sholevar (Ed.), *The handbook of marriage and marital therapy.* New York: SP Medical and Scientific Books.

Spark, G. (1974). Grandparents and intergenerational family therapy. *Family Process,* 13, 225-238.

Spark, G. (1981). Marriage is a family affair: An intergenerational approach to marital therapy. In G. Sholevar. (Ed.), *The handbook of marriage and marital therapy.* New York: SP Medical and Scientific Books.

Stanton, M. (1978). Some outcome results and aspects of structural family therapy with drug addicts. In D. Smith, S. Anderson, M. Buxton, T. Chung, N. Gottlieb, W. Harvey, (Eds.), *A multicultural view of drug abuse.* Cambridge: Schenkman.

Stanton, M. (1980). Family therapy: Systems approaches. In G. P. Sholevar, R.M. Benson and B.J. Blinder (Eds.), *Emotional disorders of children and adolescents: Medical psychological approaches to treatment.* Jamaica, N.Y.: Medical and Scientific Books.

Stanton, M. (1981). Strategic approaches to family therapy. In A.S. Gurman and D.P. Kniskern (Eds.), *Handbook of family therapy.* New York: Brunner/Mazel.

Steinglass, P. (1978). The conceptualization of marriage from a systems theory perspective. In T.J. Paolino and B.S. McCrady (Eds.), *Marriage and marital therapy: Psychoanalytic, behavioral and systems theory perspectives.* New York: Brunner/Mazel.

Stephan, T. & Markman, H. (1983). Assessing the development of relationships: A new measure. *Family Process,* 23(1), 5-25.

Stuart, R. (1976). Operant-interpersonal treatments for martial discord. In D. Olson (Ed.), *Treating relationships.* Lake Mills, IA: Graphic Press.

Stuart, R. (1980). *Helping Couples Change.* New York: Guilford.

Watzlawick, P., Beavin, J., Jackson, D. (1967). *Pragmatics of human communication: A study of interactional patterns, pathologies, and paradoxes.* New York: W.W. Norton.

Watzlawick, P., Weakland, J., Fisch, R. (1974). *Change: Principles of problem formation and problem resolution.* New York: W.W. Norton.

Weakland, J., Fisch, R., Watzlawick, P., Bodin, A. (1974). Brief therapy: focused problem resolution. *Family Process,* 13, 141-168.

Weiss, R., Hops, H., Patterson, G. (1973). A framework for conceptualizing marital conflict, a technology for altering it, and some data for evaluating it. In L. Hamerlynch, C. Handy, E. Mash (Eds.) *Behavior change: methodology, concepts, and practice.* Champaign: Research Press.

Whitaker, C. (1978). Cotherapy of chronic schizophrenia. In M. Berger (Ed.), *Beyond the double bind: Communication and family systems, theories & techniques with schizophrenics.* New York: Brunner/Mazel.

Whitaker, C., Greenberg, A., Greenberg, M. (1981). Existential marital therapy: A synthesis. In G. Sholevar (Ed.) *The handbook of marriage and marital therapy.* New York: Spectrum.

Willi, J. (1984). The concept of collusion: A combined systemic-psychodynamic approach to marital therapy. *Family Process,* 23:177-185.

Winnicott, D. (1965). *The maturational process and the facilitating environment* London: Hogarth.

The Role of Structure
in Couples Therapy:
A Search for Universal Threads

Lynn Pearlmutter

SUMMARY. The universal thread of the therapist's use of structure in the beginning, middle and termination phases of couples therapy is explored across different theoretical models. The uses of history, intensity, skill building, and unconscious material are among the topics considered. Also briefly raised are such issues as decisions about individual and/or conjoint sessions, use of explicit goal setting, and when to focus on extramarital affairs.

Thinking about the role of structure, the regulation of intensity and the sequencing of phase specific interventions, can organize the search for universal threads in couples therapy. Many diverse methods and interventions are available from which to choose and the decisions made can be critical to the success of the therapy. Heuristically couples therapists can be grouped into three broad groups: (a) those who expect the clients to take the initiative for the content of all interviews, (b) those who would provide clear and explicit structure throughout the therapy and (c) those who would weave back and forth between leading the clients and letting the clients lead.

GETTING STARTED

Choices made in the first minutes of the initial interview may lay the foundation for the future satisfaction levels of the partners (Hieb-

Lynn Pearlmutter, DSW, is Assistant Professor at Tulane University, School of Social Work. She is a Board Certified Diplomate in Clinical Social Work who in her private practice specializes in couples therapy.

ert & Gillespie, 1984; Kantor, 1985). Several couples therapists discuss the importance of a structured, practical, authoritative approach beginning in the first interview in order to prevent the clients from fumbling and to prevent the frustrated feelings that will emerge if the therapist is not "in charge" (Satir, 1965; Stuart, 1980; Beavers, 1985a). Greene (1965) believes the clients need to experience hope as early as the first ten minutes.

Other marital therapists advocate watching the couple interact with a minimum of interference. A psychoanalytically oriented marital therapist will be more inclined to let the couple begin the session and will structure the time minimally (Dare, 1986). Young-Eisendrath (1984) asks the partners to talk with each other just as they did in the car while traveling to the clinician's office. She then observes this interaction for 10 to 15 minutes. Another popular opener reported is, "What seems to be the problem?" (Framo, 1982); followed by "What have you done about the problem to date?" (Kantor, 1985). Yalom (1989) asks, "What ails?"

The therapist models effective communication from the outset of the therapy. Since "it is impossible NOT to communicate" (Lederer & Jackson, 1968, p. 99), communication interventions begin during the first moments of the therapy. Partners can be asked to speak directly to each other as opposed to talking directly to the therapist. Another early communication intervention is to suggest to the couple that in general the interview will proceed more smoothly if each speaks for himself/herself and avoids the word "we" (Framo, 1982).

Frequently clinicians allot more time for the first interview; up to two hours is reported. Subsequent interviews will then follow a more traditional therapeutic hour (Gurman, 1985; Byng-Hall, 1985). The therapist needs to outline the time-frames of the therapy in the first session (Todd, 1986).

In addition to disagreements on the importance of structure in the first interview, similarly varied opinions exist in the literature on quantity of information to be gathered during the crucial initial interview. Framo (1982) seeks maximum information; many therapists will devote several sessions exclusively to history gathering and assessment (Kaslow, 1985; Stream, 1985; Jacobson & Holtzworth-Munroe, 1986). Haley (1963) will not focus on history or assessment;

Stuart (1980) gathers only that information which he considers neces-sary and sufficient.

Courtship is often considered a source of many of the unmet ex-pectations, needs and disappointments in a relationship. Information about the courtship/dating experience is sought both by therapists gathering maximum history and by those seeking only minimal back-ground (Lederer & Jackson, 1968; Ables, 1977; Stuart, 1980; Hiebert & Gillespie, 1984; Byng-Hall, 1985). Since the courtship phase often includes many pleasant memories for a couple, accessing the positive feelings that were experienced during that stage of the relationship may begin an orientation that will assist the couple in moving from an exclusive focus on the negative aspects of the relationship.

Engaging the Couple in Treatment

Engaging the couple, sometimes described as "joining," is a criti-cal first session intervention if the clients are to return for future sessions. The processes involved in engaging a couple include em-pathic responses, accommodating to the feedback from the couple, observing the couple's "dance" and learning to move with their rhythm and steps. Once a therapeutic milieu is created and a stage is set for cooperation, the clinician will be in a position to help the couple change (Martin, 1976; Stream, 1985; Todd, 1986; Treadway, 1985; de Shazer & Berg, 1985). Some believe that the therapist's primary task is to motivate the clients by determining what they do and do not want, and then demonstrating to them that he/she will be able to teach them to "get what they want and avoid what they do not want" (Guerney, Brock & Coufal, 1986, p. 170).

Goal Setting

Frequently goal setting is a means of further engaging and motivat-ing couples. Clinicians of many persuasions have agreed on the value of goal setting; therapists vary on the types of goals to be recom-mended (Satir, 1965; Mudd & Goodwin, 1965; Ackerman, 1965; Stuart, 1980; Liberman, Wheeler, deVisser, Kuehnel & Kuehnel, 1980; Framo, 1982; Willi, 1982; L'Abate & McHenry, 1983; Pittman, 1983; Byng-Hall, 1985; de Shazer & Berg, 1985; Kantor, 1985; Stanton, 1985; Sager, 1986; Jacobson & Holtzworth-Munroe, 1986; Todd, 1986; Baucom & Hoffman, 1986). The majority of marital therapists surveyed reported working with goals related to the improvement of communication skills (Sprenkle & Fisher, 1980). Cognitive/behavioral therapists organize their goals to increase the ratio of positive to negative behavior exchanges. Marital therapists whose orientation focuses upon the family of origin will state goals in terms of helping clients with differentiation of self and helping the partners to decrease their reactivity to relationship issues which result from legacies or loyalties in the families of origin (Bowen, 1978; Boszormenyi-Nagy & Krasner, 1986).

Some couples therapists are quite explicit in the goal-setting process. Proponents of time-limited therapy emphasize a goal-directed focus with concrete, specific behavioral terminology (de Shazer & Berg, 1985). A written, signed goal setting sheet is considered an essential means of motivating clients to change (Stuart, 1980).

With some couples setting goals is straightforward. With others, the partners want to define the problem as the mate's responsibility. Framing the problem to convince the couple that their problems are solvable and that the relationship issues are a mutual responsibility is a prerequisite for further interventions (Todd, 1986; Jacobson & Holtzworth-Munroe, 1986). The therapist must join with the couple's goals or the treatment plan will not be accepted. Nor is it sufficient merely to set goals. The clinician needs to keep the therapy goal-focused.

Ending the First Interview

Many therapists will end the first session with the goal setting as a map for future sessions. Therapists who emphasize assessment and information gathering in the initial stage of couples treatment are reluctant to intervene with skill-building techniques until a much later stage of therapy (Framo, 1982; Hiebert & Gillespie, 1984; Kaslow, 1986). Stream (1985) believes that couples often need several interviews to discuss their doubts about being in treatment. The opposing perspective is that the best way to approach a couple's hesitancy is to initiate a change process immediately. In order to complete the engagement process, positive changes must occur during the first interview (Jacobson & Holtzworth-Munroe, 1986). Therapeutic tenacity is needed to implement an early change process. In order to produce the rapid change he believes clients need, Stuart (1980) introduces an extensive structured "caring days intervention" which is set up during the first interview, assigned as homework and then reviewed in the second interview as a prerequisite for further therapeutic intervention.

SECOND INTERVIEW

The debate over the role of structure continues beyond the first interview. Alan Gurman (1985), a proponent of structure in the initial interview, then relaxes this method during the second interview to allow the couple to begin to take ownership of the therapy. Lieberman and Lieberman (1986) warn that if the therapist does not continue to structure the therapy after the first interview a pattern will emerge where the couple will begin telling the story of the "week that was." Other clinicians continue to gather assessment and history information through the second and third interviews and beyond.

COMBINING INDIVIDUAL SESSIONS
WITH JOINT SESSIONS

Scharff and Scharff (1991) discuss the advantages and disadvantages of combining individual sessions with partners with the conjoint process. The advantages of seeing a partner alone include the therapist gathering increased information about secrets, feelings and opinions. The disadvantages of individual interviews include that the therapist can be burdened with knowing information which then cannot be used in joint sessions thereby inhibiting the therapist's spontaneity and maneuverability to speculate freely out loud with the couple. Scharff and Scharff state that either exclusively conjoint or conjoint combined with individual sessions can work.

COMMUNICATION SKILL BUILDING

One of the most universal ways that marital therapists help couples to change is through improvement of communication skills. Benignly attributing a couple's difficulties to a skill deficit problem can help reverse their sense of futility and despair (Jacobson & Holtzworth-Munroe, 1986). A pioneer in conjoint marital therapy, Virginia Satir (1965) wrote about the pain a couple feels as a result of dysfunctional communication processes. Beavers (1985a) discussed how helping a couple to observe their own stereotyped patterns which he calls "spin-outs" can be part of the initial phase of therapy.

Training needs to include both verbal/nonverbal and receptive/expressive domains of communication (Liberman et al, 1980; Jacobson & Holtzworth-Munroe, 1986) and needs to proceed one step at a time. The literature abounds with specific suggestions and techniques for helping couples improve communication skills. Ables (1977), Liberman et al (1980), Stuart (1980), Sherman & Fredman (1986) among many others provide the couples therapist with specific communication skill building recommendations which will not be repeated here. The communication skill building phase of therapy is largely educative and may be the most structured and directive phase of therapy (Jacobson & Holtzworth-Munroe, 1986).

Although universally agreeing on the importance of good communication, conjoint marital therapists may disagree about the premise for good communications within the therapeutic context. Framo (1982) believes that sometimes partners agree to come to couples therapy so they can find a safe environment to tell their mates what they really feel or think. Mudd and Goodwin (1965) promote communication for "deeper" understandings. The human potential movement which inspired many therapists espoused tenets of open and honest communication (Schutz, 1967).

Stuart (1980) cautions against encouraging "negative" communications because such feedback may be change inhibiting. He advocates for "norms of measured honesty" (p. 220). A relationship may be too fragile to bear uncensored open communication. Too much information can "pierce the illusions that usually help to foster feelings of love" (p. 219). Lansky (1986) also cautioned that communication is not always a "relief and opportunity; it is often a mortification and a real danger" (p. 573). Not only is one partner capable of shaming the other but the therapist under the guise of enhancing client responsibility can also trigger shame which may lead to interrupted

treatment. The shame issues are particularly relevant with narcissisti-
cally vulnerable persons.

MIDDLE PHASE

Improved communication techniques alone do not remove the
structural inflexibilites in a relationship. Any hope gained from
improved communication skills can quickly deteriorate into dis-
couragement. By this time, the couple is well into what is usually
referred to as "middle phase," which is a stage of treatment which
presents its own structural considerations. The therapist is advised
to take responsibility for any setbacks as a means of keeping the
couple engaged in treatment (Treadway, 1985). Another danger is
that the therapist will overregulate. The therapist needs to avoid
participating in the couples' real-life decisions (Jacobson & Holtzworth-Munroe, 1986; Whitaker, 1982). Both the therapist and the
couple need to practice forbearance in order to reach this stage. As
discussed above caution is advised throughout the literature on
marital therapy regarding the premature expression of negativity
between partners. In earlier stages of the therapy, the clinician
needs to acknowledge the negative feelings when they are expressed, demonstrate understanding of the feelings, insist that collaborative behavior continue despite these feelings and promise
future opportunity to deal with the negativity (Jacobson & Holtzworth-Munroe, 1986). When an issue is so "hot" that it becomes a
constant distractor for the therapist as well as the couple it is sometimes essential to ignore it at least temporarily or to relegate this to a
subordinate role. It may be a behavior so pervasive and entrenched
that it detracts from the change position (Feldman, 1986). Solomon
(1989) works from a slow, long-term model where the therapy is
perceived as a "safe-haven, to contain negative affects that invariably
emerge, and to keep them from becoming destructive"
(p. 137).

Structural Inflexibilities

By this stage of the therapy, a couple's rigid unsatisfying "patterns
of obligatory repetition" are evident through observations (Waring,

1988, p. 41). The cycles of recursive behavior prevent crisis resolution and maintain marital dissatisfaction. Bader and Pearson (1988) present a view of structural inflexibilities through a developmental model which classifies each partner as being in (a) symbiosis, (b) differentiation, (c) practicing, (d) rapprochement, or (e) mutual interdependence. Interventions are then planned for each couple's unique combination of developmental stages.

Pittman (1987) believes these structural patterns fall into one of two categories: (a) problems of being too dangerously close or (b) problems of being underinvolved. Before further intervention, a redefining of the pattern as one of the above with the couple is critical. Helping the couple see the pattern reframed as their attempted solution gives the problem a positive connotation which will activate their collaborative stance as they move into seeking new solutions (Liberman et al, 1980). Kantor (1985) seeks a transformation of the "internalized meaning structures that each partner has used as a basis for the part he or she plays in creating and maintaining the problematic sequence" (p. 24). Agreeing that couples play out redundant patterns, the analytic marital therapist's intervention would be to confront, clarify and interpret the pattern (Stream, 1985).

Anger Reduction

A range of belief systems exists among couples therapists regarding the expression of anger. Some believe that anger must always be expressed while others believe that anger should never be expressed. Most therapists take a moderate view. Anger reduction interventions can be a critical aspect of conflict resolution. Increased intimacy will not always be the byproduct of conflict resolution. Attempts to resolve the conflict may also lead to further distance between partners and an unsuccessful resolution may lead to the dissolution of the marriage (L'Abate & McHenry, 1983).

Stuart (1980) posits that an unchecked opportunity to rehash "dirty laundry lists" (p. 69) will not produce change and that " . . . a search for roots of conflict in the past should be abandoned in favor of the quest for solutions in the present" (p. 291). Rather than nourish the anger, the therapist can help the couple to weaken the anger. Greenberg and Johnson (1986) both agree and disagree with Stuart. They agree that an unchecked emotional discharge of often repeated resentments and sadness is dysfunctional "because it may entrench already destructive patterns of escalation" (p. 273). Greenberg and Johnson, unlike Stuart, seek the "previously unexpressed resentment or the buried sadness" as an aid to problem solving and intimacy building (p. 259). As with communication skills, the literature abounds with specific suggestions for helping couples de-escalate anger (Young-Eisendrath, 1984; Liberman et al, 1980; Treadway, 1985).

Power Struggles

Another structural inflexibility seen by marital therapists is couples locked into power struggles. Beavers (1985a) observes that both dominant and submissive partners are equally trapped in the struggle. A variation on the power struggle theme is a relationship organized around one spouse's being strong and the other weak or one being well and the other being sick (Treadway, 1985). Marital satisfaction increases when a couple develops a management structure which shares the level of dominance in the relationship (Rogers & Bagarozzi, 1983). Issues of power and authority are central to Stuart's (1980) concepts on how to help couples change; his goal is to help the couple achieve a power structure which is defined and flexible.

Methods of problem solving called win/win or no-lose problem solving are frequently introduced to couples locked into power struggles as well as those with more subtle problems of power and dominance. This is another form of skill building which helps to build up a couple's behavioral muscles (Nichols, 1985). Universal agreement on the benefits of problem solving methods does not exist. Problem solving methods are aspects of a basically instrumental, linear paradigm which may not be comprehensive enough to deal with all the complex features of a couples interaction. Transferring communication and problem solving skills to real life situations provides a challenge for both the therapist and the couple (L'Abate & Mc Henry, 1983).

The Unconscious Marital Patterns

Clifford Sager (1976) articulated the explication of conscious and unconscious contracts within a couple's relationship which forces the couple and the therapist to look beyond the linear, instrumental features of a marriage. To focus upon the unconscious forces within a marriage, a myriad of other methods of assessment and therapeutic interventions have been developed.

One common unconscious process observed between couples is a destructive externalization pattern called projective identification. Originally described by analyst Melanie Klein (1956) as a defense in the context of object relations, projective identification as used by spouses was first described by Dicks (1967). Many therapists since Dicks have continued to view projective identification as a central theme in their couples work. Beavers (1985b) describes this process of projective identification as the "unholy bargain" a couple negotiates. What one spouse is "claiming to be actions, feelings, dynamics, or defenses of the mate" may be disowned and the attributes camouflaged through the use of projective identification (Martin, 1975, p. 251). Clients will sabotage behavior prescriptions if the unconscious patterns are not dealt with by the therapist. The success of marital therapy is contingent upon the therapist's ability to sensitize the clients to the insight that chronic marital complaints are recapitulations of "unconscious neurotic childhood conflicts" (Stream, 1985, p. 251).

Aylmer (1986) discusses how these externalizations may be the product of a multigenerational family projection process. The spouses came out of their families of origin "programmed to reenact roles and characteristics belonging to people, relationships and events long buried" (p. 116). Individuals develop "emotional addictions" and "emotional allergies" from their families of origin which become displaced onto the marriage. The major goal of therapy is to neutralize these toxic issues and leave spouses with "less unfinished business, fewer unrealistic expectations and more ability to tolerate differences" (p. 135). Lay writer Maggie Scarf has explicated the projective identification process in her book *Intimate Partners* (1987); when the use of bibliotherapy is appropriate, this book is recommended for couples engaged in projective identification. The goal as stated by L'Abate and McHenry (1983) is to enable partners to see themselves more objectively with less projection, less destructive aggression, and an ability to manage their ambivalence (L'Abate & McHenry, 1983). Beavers (1985b) believes that the family of origin exploration helps people to accept the experience of mixed feelings and helps to unlock stuck and stubborn patterns.

Family of Origin

If the therapist focuses on a couple's covert process too soon when the couple is in crisis, the therapist disturbs the couple's interpersonal interactions which need no further agitation. Long-term change would require interventions addressing blocked family of origin displacements. Otherwise the couple could relapse and return to crisis. If too much emphasis is put on the family of origin at the beginning of therapy, clients fail to see its relevance to the intense immediate problems which they present to the therapist. Later in the therapy one or both spouses usually become motivated to work on their unresolved emotional attachments to their families of origin (Bockus, 1980; Kerr, 1985). Williamson and Allen (1984) believe that the therapist cannot address the underlying issues with a couple unless communication training, behavior contracting and structural assessments are used first as a means of stabilizing the couple.

The question then is not whether to gather family history but how much history to collect and when to begin (Moultrop, 1985). Because of their strong belief in the impact of intergenerational issues on the problems between couples, many marital therapists are inclined to begin therapy with the gathering of intergenerational history information (Framo, 1982; Bowen, 1978). Dare (1986) briefly delays the exploration of childhood origins of current conflicts and then introduces it in order to dissipate a persistent quarrel and help build empathy between spouses. Many therapists assign family of origin work to the last phase of therapy (Treadway, 1985).

Marital therapists frequently gather historical information through the use of the genogram (Dare, 1986; Treadway, 1985). The genogram is an "annotated family tree . . . a common calendar time frame allowing rapid access to and retrieval of important data" (Aylmer, 1986, p. 119). It has also been described as a "roadmap of the family relationship system" (Sherman & Fredman, 1986, p. 83). The therapist is looking for themes of triangles, justice, boundaries, emotional cutoffs, overinvolvements, family myths and skeletons as well as facts such as sibling position, education, occupation, ethnicity, religion, death, illness and great success. Completing the genogram is seen not only as a powerful assessment tool but as an intervention which may itself help the couple to reduce anxiety, change triangular patterns and repair cutoffs (Lansky, 1986; Guerin, Fay, Burden & Kautto, 1987; Byng-Hall, 1985; Sherman & Fredman, 1986).

Gathering history through the genogram has also been described as a process of "reattribution of discord." Learning one's own and one's spouse's personal history can be a convincing and constructive externalization for behavior patterns which are a source of blame and guilt (Revensorf, 1984). Family of origin interventions are not initiated by the therapist to create behavior change but rather with a view to changing the couple's perspective (Kantor, 1985).

Lansky (1987) states that the intergenerational approach can be a tool to minimize shame and to see marital problems in perspective. Partners who are desperate and easily humiliated can be helped through a focus on the family of origin. The process of unfolding family of origin themes usually begins with the genogram and leads to other methods.

Framo (1982) believes the therapist needs to be eclectic in choice of family of origin techniques. Beavers (1985a) has given some of these other techniques such clever names as: eyewitness, field trips, inviting the natives to tea, case studies (i.e., bringing the family of origin into treatment) and data analysis. When people are sent home again to their family of origin or to a cemetery they may benefit by getting some distance from the terror of their marriages. They may begin to see themselves as others see them (Pittman, 1983). An enactment that invokes the past or an evocative sculpture can give the couple a new peak experience, leaving them altered in a way that defies logical description. Often the change is experienced as magical or sensory rather than cognitive. A cognitive or perceptual reassemblage may result after the therapeutic crisis (Kantor, 1985).

Murray Bowen (1978) originated the approach to couples which focuses specifically on coaching each partner to return home to facilitate a differentiation of self from the family of origin. James Framo (1982), a pioneer in working with couples, often brings each spouse's family of origin into a conjoint family therapy marathon weekend session. Prior to the family of origin interview, the client is coached in observing himself and his family objectively and thereby gaining control over "emotional reactivity" to his family. Both Framo's and Bowen's approaches are seen as long-term approaches to working with couples. Although the fusion with family of origin may become dormant after leaving home, it is usually far from being resolved. Even small changes toward resolving the attachments to the family of origin can produce profound changes in the individual. When a couple has irresolvable struggles which end up in impasses or a win/loss, a differentiation of self orientation can provide a path to take the focus off the problem and allow for thoughtful explorations (Kerr, 1985).

Other Techniques

Williamson and Allen (1984), Framo (1982) and Grunenbaum (1985) are among those couples therapists who believe a couples group may be the best way to structure intervention. Many other techniques are used to break rigid patterns with couples. An overly intellectualized or nonverbalizing couple might benefit from interventions such as sculpture, choreography, metaphor, spatializations and time lines (Kantor, 1985; Papp, 1983). The use of the "double," a shadow-self, can help clients to express feelings they cannot otherwise express. Role reversals and trading places can also be implemented (Young-Eisendrath, 1984). To deal with old hurts, couple therapists frequently prescribe rituals as a means to bring closure to old wounds (Imber-Black, 1988).

Affairs

Constantine (1986) states that in some situations extramarital sexuality may be "irrelevant to the treatment or even positive and a beneficial part of the relationship" (p. 412). If such is the case the advice is "if it works, don't fix it" (p. 416). When the therapist chooses or if one or both partners force a focus on issues around extramarital affairs, it is best deferred for this stage of the therapy. The therapist will want to determine the meaning of the affair to the relationship and prepare interventions accordingly (Brown, 1991). Generally it is believed that an extramarital affair is indicative of a "complicated set of interlocking, invisible loyalties and disloyalities. The affair is disloyal to the marriage. The marriage may be disloyal to the family of origin"

(Boszormenyi-Nagy & Krasner, 1986, p. 338). Frequently rituals are used to try to bring closure to an old affair that has never been resolved by the couple (Imber-Black, 1988).

TERMINATION

Little has been written about ending therapy, and information on ending couples therapy is scarce. The therapist wants to promote a "good ending" with some attempts at closure. If the focus of the couples therapy has been more interactive than transferential, one or two sessions are usually sufficient. The amount of time spent terminating the therapy will usually be proportional to the time spent in the therapeutic process. Often couples begin to schedule appointments less frequently as they begin to reach their goals. A preplanned follow-up appointment scheduled ahead for several months after the formal therapy has ended has been used with good results (Weeks,1989). A therapeutic process that begins with informal or formal goal setting will certainly include a "goal review" as part of this good ending. Couples may end therapy without necessarily having made a final decision about reconciliation, separation, or other structural changes. At a minimum, the therapist needs to acknowledge that the contracted number of sessions has ended and that the therapist is available, if needed, for future sessions.

CONCLUSION

In summary, as suggested by Beavers (1985a) and reconstructed throughout this discussion, couples need three kinds of help: (a) new learning, (b) awareness of patterned behavior and (c) clarity of confusion between then and now. A wide variety of therapeutic interventions has been described which includes all three categories. Not all therapists would agree upon the equal importance or ordering of the above list. In addition to the usual therapeutic skills, the couples therapist's skillful choices, ability to teach when needed and to time the three kinds of help will be instrumental in providing the couple with the opportunity for an improved relationship. A structured but flexible framework for couples therapy is critical if the therapist is to practice forbearance. Without structure, the therapeutic process will be unfocused, emotionally laden material may quickly and prematurely escalate into untherapeutic negativity and the clients will likely terminate before an adequate exploration of change possibilities has begun.

Although "the map is not the territory" (Bateson, 1972, p. 449), having an itinerary, a structured plan which allows some room for spontaneity, may be the essential tool. Without the map the therapist may get lost in content. The consequence of the therapist's being lost is that the couples redundant patterns will persist and they will be unable to explore new territory. With a map, the couples therapist will be better prepared to implement a change process for those troubled couples who seek help with their relationship.

REFERENCES

Ables, B. S. in collaboration with Brandsma, J. M. (1977). *Therapy for couples.* San Francisco: Jossey-Bass.

Ackerman, N. W. (1965). The family approach to marital disorders. In B. L. Greene (Ed.), *The psychotherapies of marital disharmony.* New York: Free Press.

Aylmer, R. C. (1986). Bowen family systems marital therapy. In N. S. Jacobson & A. S. Gurman (Eds.), *Clinical handbook of marital therapy* (pp. 107-150). New York: Guilford.

Bader, E. & Pearson, P. T. (1988). *In quest of the mythical mate.* New York: Brunner/Mazel.

Bateson, G. (1972). *Steps to an ecology of mind.* New York: Ballantine.

Baucom, D. H. and Hoffman, J. A. (1986). The effectiveness of marital therapy: Current status and applications to the clinical setting. In N. S. Jacobson & A. S. Gurman (Eds.), *Clinical handbook of marital therapy* (pp. 597-620). New York: Guilford.

Beavers, W. R. (1985a). *Successful marriage.* New York: W. W. Norton.

Beavers, W. R. (1985b). Marital therapy in a family plagued with physical illness. In A. S. Gurman (Ed.), *Casebook of marital therapy* (pp. 177-198). New York: Guilford.

Bockus, F. (1980). *Couple therapy.* New York: Jason Aronson.

Bowen, M. (1978). *Family therapy in clinical practice.* New York: Jason Aronson.

Boszormenyi-Nagy, I. & Krasner, B. R. (1986). *Between give and take.* New York: Brunner/Mazel.

Brown, E.M. (1991). *Patterns of infidelity and their treatment.* New York: Brunner/Mazel.

Byng-Hall, J. (1985). Resolving distance conflicts. In A. S. Gurman (Ed.), *Casebook of marital therapy* (pp. 1-20). New York: Guilford.

Constanine, L. L. (1986). Jealousy and extramarital sexual relations. In N. S. Jacobson & A. S. Gurman (Eds.), *Clinical handbook of marital therapy* (pp. 407-428). New York: Guilford.

Dare, C. (1986). Psychoanalytic marital therapy. In N. S. Jacobson & A. S. Gurman (Eds.), *Clinical handbook of marital therapy* (pp. 13-28). New York: Guilford.

deShazer, S. & Berg, I. (1985). A part is not apart: Working with only one of the partners present. In A. S. Gurman (Ed.), *Casebook of marital therapy* (pp. 97-110). New York: Guilford.

Dicks, H. V. (1967). *Marital tensions*. New York: Basic Books.

Feldman, L. B. (1986). Sex-role issues in marital therapy. In N. S. Jacobson & A. S. Gurman (Eds.), *Clinical handbook of marital therapy* (pp. 345-359). New York: Guilford.

Framo, J. L. (1982). *Explorations in marital and family therapy*. New York: Springer.

Greene, B. L. (1965). *The psychotherapies of marital disharmony*. New York: Free Press.

Greenberg, L. S. & Johnson. S. B. (1986). Emotionally focused couples therapy. In N. S. Jacobson & A. S. Gurman (Eds.), *Clinical handbook of marital therapy* (pp. 253-278). New York: Guilford.

Grunenbaum, H. (1985) Inside the group. In A. S. Gurman (Ed.), *Casebook of marital therapy* (pp. 73-96). New York: Guilford.

Guerin, P. J., Fay, L. F., Burden, S. L., & Kautto, J.G. (1987). *The evaluation and treatment of marital conflict*. New York: Basic Books.

Guerney, B., Jr., Brock, G., & Coufal, J. (1986). Integrating marital therapy and enrichment: The relationship enhancement approach. In N. S. Jacobson & A. S. Gurman (Eds.), *Clinical handbook of marital therapy* (pp. 151-172). New York: Guilford.

Gurman, A. S. (1985). Tradition and transition: A rural marriage in crisis. In A. S. Gurman (Ed.), *Casebook of marital therapy* (pp. 303-336). New York: Guilford.

Haley, J. (1963). Marriage therapy. *Archives of General Psychiatry, 8*, 213-234.

Hiebert, W. J. & J. P. Gillespie. (1984). The initial interview. In R. Stahmann & W. J. Hiebert (Eds.), *Counseling in marital and sexual problems* (pp. 17-34). New York: D. C. Heath.

Imber-Black, E. (1988). Normative and therapeutic rituals in couples therapy. In E. Imber-Black, J. Roberts, & R. Whiting (Eds.), *Rituals in families and family therapy* (pp. 113-134). New York: W.W. Norton.

Jacobson, N. S. & Holtzworth-Munroe, A. (1986). Marital therapy: A social learning-cognitive perspective. In N. S. Jacobson & A. S. Gurman (Eds.), *Clinical handbook of marital therapy* (pp. 29-70). New York: Guilford.

Kantor, D. (1985). Couples therapy, crisis induction, and change. In A. S. Gurman (Ed.), *Casebook of marital therapy* (pp. 21-72). New York: Guilford.

Kaslow, F. W. (1985). To marry or not: Treating a living-together couple in midlife.

In A. S. Gurman (Ed.), *Casebook of marital therapy* (pp. 337-368). New York: Guilford.

Kerr, M. E. (1985). Obstacles to differentiation of self. In A. S. Gurman (Ed.),*Casebook of marital therapy* (pp. 111-154). New York: Guilford.

Klein, M. (1956). On identification. In M. Klein, D. Hermann, & R. E. Money-Kyrle (Eds.), *New directions in psychoanalysis*. New York: Basic Books.

Lansky, M. R. (1986). Marital therapy for narcissistic disorders. In N. S. Jacobson & A. S. Gurman (Eds.), *Clinical handbook of marital therapy* (pp. 557-574). New York: Guilford.

L'Abate, L. & McHenry. S. (1983). *Handbook of marital interventions*. New York: Grune & Stratton.

Lederer, W. & Jackson, D. D. (1968). *The mirages of marriage*. New York: Norton & Co.

Liberman, R. P., Wheeler, E. G., deVisser, L. A., Kuehnel, J. & Kuehnel, T. (1980). *Handbook of marital therapy*. New York: Plenum.

Lieberman, E. J. & Lieberman, S. B. (1986). Couples group therapy. In N. S. Jacobson & A. S. Gurman (Eds.), *Clinical handbook of marital therapy* (pp. 237-252). New York: Guilford.

Martin, P. (1976). *A marital therapy manual*. New York: Brunner/Mazel.

Moultrup, D. J. (1985). Alone together. In A. S. Gurman (Ed.), *Casebook of marital therapy* (pp. 229-252). New York: Guilford.

Mudd, E. H. & Goodwin, H. M. (1965). Counseling couples in conflicted marriages. In B. L. Greene (Ed.), *The psychotherapies of marital disharmony* (pp. 27-37). New York: Free Press.

Nichols, W. C. (1985). Differentiating couples: Some transgenerational issues in marital therapy. In A. S. Gurman (Ed.), *Casebook of marital therapy* (pp. 199-228). New York: Guilford.

Papp, P. (1983). *The process of change*. New York: Guilford.

Pittman, F. S. (1987). *Turning points*. New York: W. W. Norton.

Revenstorf, D. (1984). The role of attribution distress in therapy. In K. Halweg & N. S. Jacobson (Eds.), *Marital interaction* (pp. 325-336). New York: Brunner/Mazel.

Rogers, L.E. & Bargarozzi, D.A. (1983). In D. A. Bagarozzi, A. P. Jurisch, & R. W. Jackson (Eds.), *New perspectives in marital and family therapy: Theory, research & practice*. New York: Human Sciences.

Sager, C. J. (1976). *Marriage contracts and couple therapy*. New York: Brunner/Mazel.

Sager, C. J. (1986). Therapy with remarried couples. In N. S. Jacobson & A. S. Gurman (Eds.), *Clinical handbook of marital therapy* (pp. 321-344). New York: Guilford.

Satir, V. (1965). Conjoint marital therapy. In B. L. Greene (Ed.), *The psychotherapies of marital disharmony*. New York: Free Press.

Scarf, M. (1987). *Intimate partners*. New York: Random House.

Scharff, D.E. & Scharff, J.S. (1991). *Object relations couple therapy*. Northvale, NJ: Jason Aronson.

Schutz, W. C. (1967). *Joy: Expanding human awareness.* New York: Grove Press.
Sherman, R. & Fredman, N. (1986). *Handbook of structured techniques in marriage and family therapy.* New York: Brunner/Mazel.
Solomon, M. F. (1989). *Narcissism and intimacy.* New York: Norton.
Sprenkle, D. H. & Fisher, B. F (1980). An empirical assessment of the goals of family therapy. *Journal of Marriage and Family Therapy, 6*(2), 131-139.
Stanton, D. (1985). The marriage contract as wolfbane, or the way we were. In A. S. Gurman (Ed.), *Casebook of marital therapy* (pp. 253-270). New York: Guilford.
Stream, H. S. (1985). *Resolving marital conflicts.* New York: John Wiley.
Stuart,7 R. B. (1980). *Helping couples change.* New York: Guilford Press.
Todd, T. C. (1986). Structural-strategic marital therapy. In N. S. Jacobson & A. S. Gurman (Eds.), *Clinical handbook of marital therapy* (pp. 71-106). New York: Guilford.
Treadway, D. C. (1985). Learning their dance: Changing some steps. In A. S. Gurman (Ed.), *Casebook of marital therapy* (pp. 155-176). New York: Guilford.
Waring, E. M. (1988). *Enhancing marital intimacy through facilitating cognitive self-disclosure.* New York: Brunner/Mazel.
Weeks, G. R. (1989). *Treating couples.* New York: Brunner/Mazel.
Whitaker, C. (1982). Functions of marriage. In J. R. Neill & D. P. Kniskern (Eds.), *From psyche to system* (pp. 166-175). New York: Guilford.
Whitaker, C. (1982). Psychotherapy with couples. In J. R. Neill & D. P. Kniskern (Eds.), *From psyche to system* (pp. 175-181). New York: Guilford.
Whitaker, C. (1982). Psychotherapy with married couples. In J. R. Neill & D. P. Kniskern (Eds.), *From psyche to system* (pp. 182-189). New York: Guilford.
Whitaker, C. (1982). Psychotherapy of marital conflict. In J. R. Neill & D. P. Kniskern (Eds.), *From psyche to system* (pp. 182-189). New York: Guilford.
Whitaker, C. & Miller, M. H. (1982). A reevaluation of "psychiatric help" when divorce impends. In. J. R. Neill & D. P. Kniskern (Eds.), *From psyche to system* (pp. 196-207). New York: Guilford.
Willi, J. (1982). *Couples in collusion.* New York: Jason Aronson.
Williamson, D. S. & Allen, F. E. (1984). Couple conflict and intergenerational consultation: The chicken that came before the egg. In R. F. Stahmann & W. J. Hiebert (Eds.), *Counseling in marital and sexual problems* (pp. 101-114). New York: D. C. Heath.
Yalom, I. (1989). *Loves's executioner.* New York: Basic Books.
Young-Eisendrath, P. (1984). *Hags and heroes.* Toronto: Inner City.

Couple Crises
and the Trigenerational Family

Maurizio Andolfi
Vincenzo F. DiNicola (translator)

SUMMARY. A trigenerational approach to couple crises is presented. Key ideas are developed from the work of Bowen, Framo and Whitaker on families of origin: Bowen sends partners back to their own families; Framo invites the extended family into the session with the couple; Whitaker enlarges the unit of observation to include more family members, increasing family resources. For the author, the early phase of therapy is diagnostic, so extended family members are invited to provide information as consultants. One couple's crisis is reviewed in detail. Issues arising from inviting the couple's parents and siblings, their children, and the value of individual sessions for the partners are examined using the trigenerational framework.

ADA: Basically, there is a change when something changes within. External reality isn't transformed, what's inside is transformed. It's difficult to say what happened during these three years; at a certain point we just felt differently. It's something very gradual. We decided to get married at fifteen, at our desks at school. We have had an emotional bond for a very long time, from before the wedding, and we were way too young. So it was

---

Maurizio Andolfi, MD, is Associate Professor, Department of Developmental Psychology, "La Sapienza" University of Rome, Italy; Scientific Director, Family Therapy Institute of Rome, and Editor, Terapia Familiare. Author's address: 15, Via Capodistria, Rome 00198, Italy.

This article is from a chapter in M. Andolfi et al. (Eds.) (1988), *La coppia in crisi*, pp. 216-232, translated by Vincenzo F. DiNicola, MPhil, MD, DipPsych, FRCP(C), Assistant Professor, Division of Child and Adolescent Psychiatry, University of Ottawa, Department of Psychiatry; Director, Family Psychiatry Service & Adolescent Day Care Programme, Royal Ottawa Hospital, Ottawa, Ontario, Canada.

very hard for each of us to find our own identity in this suffocating marital relationship. When we landed in therapy, it was the last straw for me, the last step before separation. I felt preyed upon, caught in a web. I had to find a way to free myself and Riccardo oppressed me with all his talk, his demands for attention.

RICCARDO: We came to therapy in the worst way, after some meetings with a friend who is a psychologist, to take the edge off the crisis. From the beginning, I was convinced that the relationship between us was all wrong. I, Riccardo, was the eternal big baby and Ada, the *mamma*. I wanted to get this big baby off my back but I couldn't succeed. I was obsessed with this idea that I was a child and that Ada acted as my *mamma*. But I came to therapy as a child, more and more desperate, until I finally understood that my desperation was about me and not about playing *bambino* and *mamma*.

This is how Ada and Riccardo described the beginning of their treatment three years later, at a follow-up session. The motivations that led Ada and Riccardo to seek therapy are paradigmatic of many couples in crisis, who after years of marriage do not know where to turn, nor how to evaluate what they have built together. What prevails is a general sense of bewilderment, suffering, and loss that leads them to an exasperation of the communicative patterns that have long become the rhythm of their relationship. Ada feels hounded and wants to escape. Riccardo scolds himself for playing the big baby, but confronts Ada's suggestion to separate, reinforcing his role as a frightened child.

What I intend to describe in this article is a trigenerational approach to what I will call, for simplicity, *couple crises*. For more than fifteen years a significant part of my clinical activities has involved troubled couples. In the last five years the number of such couples requesting therapy in Italy has increased spectacularly.

KEY IDEAS

From my first encounter with Murray Bowen at Georgetown University in Washington, D.C., at the end of 1972, I was struck by his profound conviction that to resolve a problem *here and now,* it is necessary to look back *there and then.* At the beginning, this reminded me of the psychoanalytic approach and its language for images. I thought about the past, about family ghosts and their influence on the understanding of individual and couple conflicts. Later, I realized that Bowen's work is much more like the trainer of a soccer team (*coach* is a word that recurs frequently in his work) than a psychoanalyst who follows the movement of his patients step by step in the long process of psychotherapy. Just as a competent coach is able to maximize the resources and potentials of individual players as part of the overall strategy for the whole team, the same can be said of Bowen (1978) who proposed his System Theory, which differs from General System Theory as described by von Bertalanffy (1968) and from the formulations of the Mental Research Institute (Watzlawick et al., 1967) and more recently those of the Milan school (Boscolo et al., 1987). However, I do not want to discuss epistemology; rather I want to limit myself to extrapolating a few of Bowen's key ideas that have so influenced the family therapy movement in the U.S.A. in the 1960s and 1970s and that have been the basis for my development as a couple and family therapist.

Bowen does not consider it useful to observe the couple's communicative patterns. He thinks that in situations of severe stress, the two partners no longer know how to interact, but end up reacting in an automatic way to each other's reactions in a kind of vicious cycle with enormous and futile expenditures of emotional energy. From these premises, Bowen places himself as an element of discontinuity between the two partners. He alone poses questions to each of them, carefully avoiding any direct exchange between them. He systematically substitutes the word *feeling* with the word *thinking,* both in the formulation of his questions and in the answers of his patients. He is convinced that the best way to get someone to make contact with their own emotional world is by blocking them from referring to any event with terms such as feeling, seeing, perceiving, and so on. By avoiding emotional exchanges in the session, Bowen encourages an individual mental search, alternatively shifting each of the partners from actively reflecting and verbally expressing themselves to a position of listening to the other partner.

Bowen's function as an "emotional watershed" is later enhanced when he asks each of them to investigate their own place within his or her family of origin. After a careful study of the family genogram, the partners are sent home again with the task of reconnecting themselves to their original group in order to learn how to separate themselves from it. This is a serious trip for therapeutic reasons, with a suitcase and clothes as needed, presented as a real search for themselves.[1] In summary, for Bowen the problems of the couple are "frozen" with the expectation that each spouse will return with greater awareness from their voyage into their respective families of origin, in order to take up the couple dialogue with better differentiation of each individual self.

For James Framo (1982), working with the family of origin is also essential, whether one is conducting individual therapy or couple and family therapy. In couple therapy, Framo prefers convening a group of a number of couples, usually working with a co-therapist. Each couple states their problems and then listens to the other couples comments. One or more meetings with the family of origin of one or both of the partners is suggested, especially when impasses arise or in advanced phases of treatment. For Framo, however, the family of origin comes into the session rather than the client going home, as for Bowen. Framo also sees the encounter with the extended family as a personal and confidential experience, and for these reasons excludes the partner, whose presence he feels might affect the content and quality of the encounter. He is nevertheless convinced that each spouse sees the extension of the sessions to the families of origin favorably, maintaining that such sessions can trigger advantages for both partners that may eventually overcome the couple's crisis.

I worked for over five years (from 1976 to 1981), with groups of many couples, using Framo's working scheme.[2] The presence of a group of couples with similar problems undoubtedly facilitates the processes of identification and group cohesiveness. Above all it gives a sense of relativity and optimism to each couple that ends up feeling useful in the solution of the others crises and to having more faith in their own personal resources. The presence of co-therapists who are also partners allows a form of *modeling* and the chance to experiment with more flexible male-female complementarily. By working with the problems presented by each couple in a multi-couple therapy group, the meetings with families of origin become an occasional event, even if they are very profitable. In my opinion, this therapeutic approach does not adequately place the couple's crisis into a trigenerational framework.

It was only my encounter with Carl Whitaker (see Neill and Kniskern, 1982) and his coherent clinical thinking that led to a meaningful turning-point in my way of thinking about and doing therapy in the last ten years. Whitaker's influence is even more important when working with couples that are especially good at restricting the range of therapeutic interventions. For Whitaker, enlarging the unit of observation to the trigenerational family has no limits, either on the horizontal (or marital) plane, or on the vertical (or parental) plane. I have often wondered what is the source of Whitaker's confidence in convening very large families in his sessions, where children are making a racket, grown-ups eye each other with hostility, and grandparents defend their children and indirectly their own branch of the family. No sooner than a family adds a new member to the session following his advice, Whitaker will declare that the family is still "too narrow" for him. Perhaps, at this point, the family is missing some far-away uncle, practically unknown to them, but considered by Whitaker as essential to understand the entire dynamic of the family. I believe that his casual manner in expanding the therapeutic system beyond every limit is connected to his capacity to maintain himself whole, that is to constantly place himself emotionally separate from the complex conflicts that emerge in the session. This distancing permits him, for example, to fall into a deep sleep in front of a couple that keeps shooting hostile messages at him during the session; or else to lie down on the ground and play with a two-year-old child, isolating himself completely from the "war" between the grownups, who hurl accusations at each other about the causes of the couple's crisis.

This apparent "I don't care" attitude is closely connected to the intensity with which he always transmits his iron-clad conviction that even a family that is apparently broken up has intact healing resources needed in order to develop and grow. In Whitaker's view, all a family needs is to want to use its resources and not to get lost in useless power plays and attempts to control each other. From this springs his therapeutic provocation, aimed at enlarging the boundaries drawn by the family, transmitting the idea that *what the family presents as all it has is always too little*.

His concept of normality derives from challenging degrees of abnormality, stages of madness, violent and destructive fantasies, and so on. If a couple arrives in therapy presenting their home as abnormal, emphasizing the causes of their crisis, it is likely that this couple will go home confused about how to define a relationship as abnormal. The causes of the crisis, so well catalogued, will be thrown to the wind and each partner will ask himself or herself, with unsuspected curiosity, questions that seem to have no connection with their current problems. Perhaps the two, who began the session by hurling accusations at each other, almost without being aware of it, will find themselves day-dreaming and asking themselves questions about their first meeting, about their engagement, about their wedding or the way she moved her hips to seduce him during the honeymoon. Suddenly, later in the session, the spouses find themselves in a dislocated time and will be able to jump even further backwards, associating their wedding with that of their parents. They will become children discovering the meaning of their births in the relationships between their respective parents.

Whitaker proposes an associative method aimed at inducing a voyage backwards through "leaps in time" that disturb the links of meaning constructed by the couple over time and reproduced with greater rigidity in stressful situations. If one can release oneself from the present, one can play so many "as ifs," running through the lines of the family story, and then come back to the present, enriched by a more fluid perception of the order of things.

FROM THE HORIZONTAL AXIS
(MARITAL PLANE) TO THE VERTICAL
AXIS (PARENTAL PLANE)

The Diagnostic Phase

To return to Bowen's image of the suitcase and of the return home, in my clinical experience I have found it useful "to let the suitcase come to therapy" by convening the family of origin in the session, rather than sending the clients back home again. This is for several reasons: especially because it seems useful for both partners to share an important and often deeply-felt experience. The physical presence of the other spouse in the session is a confirmation that, even if indirectly, they are working on the couple's problems. It allows them, moreover, to evaluate the capacity of the partners to explain themselves in front of each other, demonstrating openly their emotional needs and old weaknesses, often concealed even after many years of living together. And above all, it is an effective way for the therapist to communicate to the partners that their families of origin are positive resources and not the cause of their problems, as is often stated by the couple. In fact, if the older generation were to perceive our request as a way to assign responsibility or blame, the effect would be damaging–the parents, feeling accused, would become extremely defensive. This often occurs regardless of our therapeutic approach, as if the parents had developed the attitude of always feeling responsible for the problems of their children, even when they are older adults. To overcome such impasses we request the presence of the parents and siblings of each partner as our consultants. The task assigned to them is to provide the therapists with useful information for a better understanding of their family member. That is, their presence is not sought out to discuss the problems of the couple, but only to get to know their child or sibling better. Their *meta*-position, supported by the therapist, enhances the search for new relational paths beyond the comfortable but futile recourse to an exchange of mutual accusations.

As we will see below in the description of the Vianini couple, the family of origin is convened in the so-called diagnostic phase of therapy, in the initial stage of treatment. At times the criticism has been voiced that we "forced the issues of the couple" without waiting for a more opportune moment to convene the families of origin. It could be argued that later in the treatment the couple would have greater confidence in the therapeutic system. In fact, this is true, but doing this would confirm the notion that the partners and their problems are the focus of therapy. The unit of observation would inevitably become the conjugal dyad, whereas the presence of the families of origin and of children in early phases quickly moves the observation to a more complete and complex unit–the family–within which the functioning and problems of the couple assume shape and meaning. Furthermore, as described below, we find it useful to increase the "vertical" or intergenerational resistance, and thus to enhance a redistribution of tension, moving it from the couple's space to the space between generations.

The proposal to enlarge the unit of observation is usually presented to the couple in concrete language. Although it has some provocative aspects, this is an understandable and clear way to offer a plan for therapy: "If you go to a doctor for some physical symptom, first a diagnosis must be made and then therapy can be prescribed. In order to formulate an accurate diagnosis, laboratory analyses are needed–blood and urine tests, X-rays, and so on. I also need some preliminary diagnostic data. Instead of blood I need your parents; rather than X-rays I must see your children and then I need to see each of you alone, not only as a couple. At the end of this exploratory phase we will look at everything and evaluate the possibility for couple therapy."

The request to bring children into the session generally elicits less concern and resistance than when parents are invited. Nevertheless it is possible that one or other of the partners will resist this request. This allows us to understand better the embarrassment of explicitly allowing children to become part of the couple's problems. Such embarrassment grows worse especially when a child has been involved in the couple's intimate space, as if they were running the risk of openly revealing how things really stand. The presence of children in the session is in any case a breath of fresh air, both for the couple and for the therapist. Children and adolescents can become useful co-therapists to the degree that we give sufficient credit to their systemic competence, developed in the family over the years. In contrast to the older generation, which acts as a catalyst for the couple's negativity, even in the most impossible couple children represent something positive that the two partners have succeeded in doing together. And this is no small thing in situations where destructiveness and mistrust prevail between a couple. Even when a child becomes the route or the messenger for the interpersonal violence of the couple, it is easier to "play" with his or her function as messenger in order to later involve the two parents.

Individual sessions for each partner elicit the least reaction. Nonetheless, the partners often find themselves in great difficulty when it becomes clear to them, during his or her individual session, that this time is reserved for each of them to talk about *him or herself before*

and outside of their marriage. In the situation of a seriously dysfunctional couple, it often occurs that neither of the two knows what to talk
about if their conjugal problems are excluded. It is as if each person's
individuality were annulled in the impossible search for a marital
context to guarantee a haven of total refuge and protection.

FROM THE "NO" OF THE COUPLE
TO THE INTERGENERATIONAL "NO"

The Vianini couple[3] requested therapy after 14 years of marriage.
The level of interpersonal tension between the two spouses was quite
intense right from the initial interactions of the first session. Laura, the
wife, was fed up and resented everything; Mario, the husband, refuted
what she said both verbally and non-verbally. Laura is a woman of 35,
well-dressed and very lively. Her shrill, loud laughter made this otherwise confidently attractive woman unpleasant. Her laughter sounded
more like howling. One sensed a lot of aggression in her, which
contrasted with the calm, controlled manner of her husband who is 15
years older and missing an arm as a result of an automobile accident.
Their interactions followed a vicious cycle in which the wife criticized
her husband, who patently denied everything she stated. Despite the
apparent willingness of both of them to talk about their marital problems, what was most striking was the uncomfortable sense of distance
and emotional coldness between them. From the beginning Marco,
their 11-year-old son, seemed to have been assigned the role of media-
tor between the two of them, confounding his needs as a child with a
pseudo-maturity and pretentiousness absolutely out of keeping with
his age.

To become involved with a couple in crisis with such a low level
of emotional availability to each other can be an exhausting and perhaps unproductive undertaking. A feeling of failure and frustration
sustains the tension that the couple brings with them into therapy. A
reasonable objective might be to reduce the tension between the two
partners, but what good is it if one does not get to the root of what is
feeding the problem? It is like administering oxygen to a dyspneic
patient without understanding the nature of the problem, of which the
dyspnea (respiratory distress) is only a symptom. If we free ourselves

of the preoccupation to soothe the crisis, we can perceive that the tension they bring into the session is the most vital interpersonal element available at the moment. If Laura were to stop howling and Mario did not respond with an equally exasperating calm, they would lose a confirmation (perhaps the only one now present) of the marital bond and its evolution over time. The task of the therapist is then to hypothesize that the couple's "mistaken" behaviors are an expression of an underlying agreement, of a genuine solidarity tested over time and now manifest in an incongruous way. It is just this meaning of solidarity that is rediscovered. The route, however, will be "indirect" and apparently unconnected to the marital crisis. The first objective is to displace the tension from the marital plane (on the horizontal axis) and to channel it towards the trigenerational plane (on the vertical axis), that includes the family of origin on the upper story and on the lower story, the children. In the case of the Vianini couple we have mentioned how Marco was precociously involved in his parent's marital problems, to the point that it is difficult to establish if they first became a couple or whether the Vianinis set up a *menage à trois* straight away.

Corresponding to a massive involvement of the son in the couple's tension, there is a distance in the couple's interactions with their respective families of origin, to the point that both categorically refuse to bring their own families into the session. The refusal of both of the spouses to an extension of the unit of observation signals the beginning of a redistribution of tension: from the couple in the center to the extended family in the periphery. Instead of getting involved in the couple's fears of further rejections and disagreements, the therapist can locate and provoke resistance linked to much more remote rejections that, if loosened, can give a more understandable meaning to the current crisis. The "no" can be expressed in many different ways, for example: "It's useless; I don't want my parents to intrude into our relationship, they never bothered themselves about my problems, I don't need anybody's help, my father is an egotist," and so on. The "no" is only apparently a denial of what is requested. If the therapist knows how to play with their "no" and its endless variations instead of blocking it, it will be easier to establish a meaningful relationship with the couple based or the areas that seem to have produced great conflict and pain for them individually and as a couple.

This then is the first path to follow in constructing the therapeutic process. The therapist is the one who can and does ask that risks be taken and that other people in the families of origin be brought into the session. The more the couple fears a meeting with the extended family, the more therapeutic such an encounter will be. The therapist is also the one who *joins in order to separate*. Tracing current relationships back to their origins and allowing bonds of dependence and affinity to emerge will bring to light the missing plot of the family story and identify common threads. Weaving together these common threads will allow the construction of a new story.

The therapist first of all asks Laura to bring her mother. Laura initially states that she is not close to her mother, "because we have such different personalities." If her refusal to let her mother participate in one of the initial sessions seems motivated by their differences, it is just as true that in expressing her dissent Laura completely changes expressions: from a snarling adolescent (as she displayed in every interaction with her husband), she appears transformed into a woman who is mature at last, marked by life and by misfortune. Her "no" now becomes a statement charged with complex and contradictory meanings that, if heeded by the therapist, can be used therapeutically. Out of fear comes the curiosity to attach herself to a territory that is still very "hot." Laura knows that if she is able to take the chance of speaking like an adult to her mother about events and relationships in the past, she may be able remove the dramatic halo through which they were seen, to reduce the ever intolerable emotional distance and recover a clearer dimension of her own identity.

When the mother does show up, all the ups and downs of the family emerge. From recounting shared suffering, mother and daughter emerge strengthened because both are more conscious of their expectations of each other and of the way in which each has sought to fill up the gaps of the other. When Laura was a child, her family had serious financial difficulties due to her father's bankruptcy. The whole family was forced to leave the Italian city where they lived, fleeing hastily to Switzerland, where thanks to a friend, Laura's father succeeded in reestablishing a good position. Her mother Rita, however, was not able to adapt herself to her new environment. Rita ardently wished to return home to be near her parents. This would probably have remained only a wish if an even more serious problem had not arisen: Laura discovered that her father was having a sexual relationship with one of her school friends. Laura, feeling doubly betrayed by her father and her friend, decided to return to Italy and her mother and brother followed her there. As a result, Laura was transformed into "the competent person" of the family, becoming a focal point and support for her mother and brother, although it was barely acknowledged by either of them. In fact, Laura learned to progressively sacrifice her own interests and aspirations in order to satisfy other people.

Through the narration of such a deeply-felt family story emerges a dependency need that had been denied continually by both of them. Since the daughter was married, the mother displayed her own independence, just as the daughter always played the role of a decisive person who takes the initiative for everybody. Such images of emotional separation and pseudoautonomy will dissolve if the mother can begin to talk about the trouble she had to face and the feeling of helplessness and loneliness she always felt; and if the mother can admit that she always sought to find a support in her daughter (although she denies it in words), and make her concealed and burdensome demands on Laura more explicit. The mother's recognition of a profound emotional void allows the daughter to recognize her own gaps better and to understand her desire to find someone (her husband, for example) who can fill them, just as she felt an obligation to fill her mother's gaps. The recognition of an impossible task in the mother-daughter relationship allows us to see other impossible tasks in the conjugal relationship, and suggests the possibility of finding more realistic and authentic alternatives for both the marital and intergenerational relationships. To the growth of intimacy between mother and daughter, there is a parallel growth in intimacy between the spouses. The fact that the husband participates as an observer of what happens between his wife and her mother gives him the chance to know his partner better and to help her solve her problems.

Mario's story is also full of rejection and suffering. His mother was an invalid who was bedridden for twenty-five years until her death. His father survived the death of his wife and "absorbed" his four sons into his business, imposing his philosophy of working together "side by side." So the children learn to neglect themselves, working in the same construction company, following the paternal edict to stay together, refusing to explore feelings of any kind in order to avoid all friction. Mario began couple therapy fully adhering to the philosophy of the father's business. The apparent calm and control with which he responds to Laura's snarling attacks is accompanied by his cordial and sometimes almost childlike facial expression. Verbally he says that therapy can only calm down his wife's impetuousness. He loses his calm and control, however, when he is asked to bring his father and his siblings to the session, as was already requested of Laura. His "no" resembles the cry of desperation of someone who must resign himself to an utter loneliness within the walls of his father's business, without even being allowed to run away.

For a number of sessions we "played" together "as if" he was telephoning his father. I would take the telephone, pull out the plug, and hand it to Mario saying, "Call him now, for a joke, with the line disconnected. Show me how many numbers you can dial before your fingers start to shake or your face turns pale." Then, I would add, "Who will speak first? What do you think your father will say when he hears your voice?" Or else, "How will you manage to get another 'no' from your father? You know, there's a way of asking that is the best way of getting a 'no.' You have learned lots of tricks for always making yourself feel rejected, after so many years of not living together. Did you notice that your son Marco is quickly learning from you not to make any demands for fear of being refused by you? This is really a family lesson. Outside the construction business, there is also a homemade lesson of no's. And your wife still persists in trying to make you say yes to her–she who has made a career of rejections." After several sessions of playing with Mario's resistance to recapturing his self-esteem, rejecting himself becomes much more embarrassing than running the risk of feeling accepted.

In my experience it is very rare that a parent who perceives an authentic request from a child would be able to refuse to deal with it. Making a request, however, means coming to terms with what Karen Horney (1950) called the *system of pride* that prefers grandiose failures (feeling like "the most neglected child in the world," for example), rather than successes of humility ("if I present myself as I really am, fragile and insecure, maybe my father will recognize and accept me for these weaknesses"). When Mario's father arrives in the session, two months after the start of therapy, one might expect a detailed report from the front lines of such a heroic undertaking. Instead it is summed up very simply: Mario made a request and his father quickly agreed. It was not only simple, but absolutely painless. In Mario's case as in the great majority of similar cases, we always wonder which version of the facts to believe: the one before the herculean attempt, or the one after which was so simple–all Mario had to do was to ask. In reality, we think that it was more difficult for Mario to accept asking within himself than being worried about a possible external rejection. The external problem is often blown out of proportion to mask the internal problem of accepting to ask, which often goes against the grain of one's own identity. To bring his father along is much more for Mario than adding another chair to the session. The same is true for the therapist, who follows a cognitive map aimed at framing the couple's problems on three generational levels. The presence of this or that family member in the session is only one working aspect of the therapist's interventions.

In this way the couple's motivations for coming into therapy are deeply changed. Now Mario's courage to re-open the door of his defensive solitude with respect to his father is also an implicit request with respect to Laura. If Mario wants to grow out of his "handicap," he cannot only change in one direction and he cannot change without renegotiating his relationship with his wife. The encounter between father and son in the presence of the therapist and Laura is partly pathetic and partly dramatic. For the first time, Laura listens attentively as someone who shares a difficult problem. While talking to his father, Mario acts like a child in search of approval; it reactivates an old stutter that makes him even more ill-at-ease. This shows how hard it is for both of them to drop the mask and reveal their own pain after so many years of "close-up distance" in the father's business. Notice the wish for a different relationship that neither of the two can ask for explicitly. The inability to ask, visibly acted out in the session, now becomes a strongly embarrassing element of unity. This embarrassment begins to loosen up their rigidified positions and to funnel them into new areas of hope for both of them.[4] In a subsequent encounter with his brothers, Mario can finally talk of his own needs. In this case, asking the brothers to come and to share some of the same difficulties can make the wall that divides them more permeable.

When meeting with families of origin, as already described by others (Boszormenyi-Nagy & Spark, 1973; Bowen, 1978; Framo,

1976; Williamson, 1981), it is essential for the encounter to end without increasing the hostility for resentment among members of the extended family. It is often wrongly thought that giving a child the chance to freely express his hidden resentment towards his parents, after having masked it for years, can help to change the relationship, so that the mother and father can have the chance to "see how things really are" for the first time. It is likely, however, that the principal expectation is to search first of all for a reparation of the relationship. The therapist must help the patient reestablish an accepting relationship with the parents. This can be obtained, not by raising old grudges and misunderstandings, but by helping the patient work out his relationship with his parents. As Williamson says,

> This rebalancing of intergenerational dynamics is the sine qua non of psychological adulthood and is the source of *personal authority* in living. The adult generation can offer support without assuming emotional responsibility or burden for the welfare, the happiness, or the survival of the aging parents. (Williamson, 1981, p. 442)

If the relationship is manifested through bitterness, it is not necessary for the individuals to reveal their ambivalence. On one hand, they feel hostility on account of their own unmet needs; on the other hand, they demand their needs to be recognized at last and to create a new relationship. This can be realized only to the degree that they discover in their disappointments–and beyond them–shared experiences, suffering, and doubts. Discovering such elements of union is preliminary to any work aimed at separating, because one cannot separate without finding the common thread.

This is the direction of our work with the families of origin of the Vianini couple. The discovery of similar experiences between Laura and her mother and between Mario and his father and his brothers is an indispensable step for the recognition of their different emotional experiences. They learn that each person's loneliness, anger, and need is different from another's and requires individual solutions. To separate oneself from the experience of one's parents, "taking distance" from them, and to accept that at least part of their story must be different from one's own story is a new insight for Laura. This will permit Laura to see even her own marriage from another perspective.

Through therapy Laura will begin to see herself in a different way, giving up her role as a nurse which denies her own needs as a woman.

A parallel movement takes place for Mario. In his case, it is overcoming his resistance to ask his brothers to attend a session that contributes to changing his relationships. For the first time a family taboo is broken. The request can be put into words; it is no longer implicit, with a tacit expectation of refusal. For the first time the brothers talk also of emotional experiences in their family of origin, they clarify Mario's experience of "invalidity" predating the accident. This contributes to exploring other aspects of his marriage, throwing light on how Mario's handicap has concretely justified his wife's role as a nurse and her unemployment outside the home, masking his long-standing emotional insecurities. All this contributes to the construction of a new marital story, where there is more room to make choices and re-establish an understanding, a vitality that is no longer burdened by old handicaps of one or the other partner.

NOTES

1. It is interesting to note that Bowen first introduced the idea of *physically* returning to one's family of origin as the best and most valuable training experience for students of family therapy. However, the issue of training, which in my opinion is crucial, is unfortunately beyond the scope of this article.

2. Each group was followed in couples therapy for two or three years, with sessions every fortnight. In this case, I conducted conjoint couple therapy with my wife, Dr. Marcella de Nichilo.

3. The case of the Vianini couple, presented in this article, appeared more extensively in our book, *The Myth of Atlas: Families and the Therapeutic Story* (Andolfi et al., 1989; see pp. 30-33, 100-110), where it was described specifically to present the construction of family myths and their evolution in therapy.

4. Eight months after this session, Mario's father died and Mario stated how important it was for him to be able to rediscover being a son after that session, before it was too late.

REFERENCES

Andolfi, M, Angelo, C., & de Nichilo, M. (1989). *The myth of Atlas: Families and the therapeutic story.* (Ed. and trans. by V.F. DiNicola.) New York: Brunner/ Mazel.

Andolfi, M, Angelo, C., & Saccu, C. (Eds.). (1988). *La coppia in crisi.* Rome: Istituto di Terapia Familiare.

Bertalanffy, L. von. (1968). *General system theory.* New York: George Braziller.

Boscolo, L., Cecchin, L., Hoffman, L., & Penn, P. (1987). *Milan systemic family therapy: Conversations in theory and practice*. New York: Basic Books.

Boszormenyi-Nagy, I., & Spark, G.M. (1973). *Invisible loyalties: Reciprocity in intergenerational family therapy*. New York: Harper & Row.

Bowen, M. (1978). *Family therapy in clinical practice*. New York: Jason Aronson.

Framo, J.L. (1982). *Explorations in marital and family therapy: Selected papers of James L. Framo*. New York: Springer.

Horney, K. (1950). *Neurosis and human growth*. New York: W.W. Norton.

Neill, J.R., & Kniskern, D.P. (Eds.). (1982). *From psyche to system: The evolving therapy of Carl Whitaker*. New York: Guilford Press.

Watzlawick, P., Beavin, J.H., & Jackson, D.D. (1967). *Pragmatics of human communication*. New York: W.W. Norton.

Williamson, D.S. (1981). Personal authority via termination of the intergenerational hierarchical boundary: A "new" stage in the family life cycle. *Journal of Marital and Family Therapy, 7(4)*, 441-452.

Life Cycle Crises:
Sources of Strain and Strength
in Relationships

Steven R. Heyman

SUMMARY. As couples are worked with in therapy, the issues they bring, both individually and as a couple, may reflect important developmental crises. This paper describes some of these issues from the perspective of Erikson's epigenetic theory. Brief case examples are provided to illustrate the presentation and therapeutic course with these issues. While these issues will present strains that bring the couple into therapy, their understanding can also provide considerable motivation for strength and growth, particularly when worked with in the therapeutic arena.

In working with couples in relationships therapists will often find that their clients' abilities to form mutually enhancing relationships will depend on more than the current situation of each of the individuals and the quality of their relationship. A great deal will depend on how they have encountered and resolved critical issues earlier in their lives, as well as how current developmental issues are experienced. This will be in terms of their ability to take the steps necessary to overcome past deficiencies and the abilities to develop the strengths necessary to create a meaningful future for themselves and in their relationships.

Psychodynamic theorists differ in the extent to which they see the past as controlling of present behavior, as well as the degree to which problems developing from past behavior can be remedied without long term, reconstructive analytic interventions. It is beyond the scope of this paper to do more than acknowledge these differences.

Steven R. Heyman is affiliated with the University of Wyoming.

Reprint requests can be sent to Steven R. Heyman, Department of Psychology, University of Wyoming, Box 3415 University Station, Laramie, WY 82071.

Erik Erikson has been one of the most influential of the analytic writers in the second half of the twentieth century. Although trained in Vienna in the 1920s as a lay analyst, he went on to become one of the foremost of the ego analysts, a group including Anna Freud, Heinz Hartmann, and Peter Blos. Although this group agreed with many of Freud's basic concepts, in general they saw the ego as stronger and more central to existence than did Freud, and they also viewed the unconscious as containing repositories of potential strengths in addition to potential sexual or aggressive conflicts.

Erikson's (1963) epigenetic theory,[1] although based on Freud's model, differs in several important ways. Freud's model has only five developmental stages. The fifth stage for Freud, the genital stage, presumably goes from puberty until death, with little attention to any but the psychosexual conflicts during these years. Erikson's theory divides the genital stage into four separate stages: adolescence, young adulthood, middle age, and older age. While Freud's theory focuses almost exclusively on psychosexual issues, Erikson stresses the importance of social and interpersonal issues. Erikson, as an ego analyst, also sees the conscious part of the mind as stronger, more capable, and more flexible than did Freud. Within this epigenetic theory, Erikson assumes that "each stage adds something specific to all later ones and makes a new ensemble out of all earlier one" (cited in Evans, 1981, p. 41). Past resolutions, for better or worse, can be modified by later events and crises (Smelser, 1980). Passage through these stages does not mean an "either-or" resolution, but rather individuals may be successful or unsuccessful in varying degrees. Erikson's theories about the life cycle, and the crisis associated with each stage, have most generally been applied to individuals, as have most analytically-oriented theories. In this paper I would like to utilize his theory, drawing on the life cycle crises, to examine themes in the relationships couples bring to therapy. Although in severe cases these can reflect pathological issues, in most cases they reflect issues in living: personal and shared developmental issues that affect individuals and couples in relationships.

The discussion that follows will identify the life cycle crises as they reflect themes likely to affect a couple's relationship. Case examples will follow, in which issues and therapeutic approaches will be described. The limitations of this paper will not allow a full examination of how these life cycle themes also become sources for strength in relationships, but some illustrations will be provided. Erikson (1964, p. 239) in discussing Freud's theory of genitality, defined this as "strivings of sexuality and love ... a partner's potency and potentialities are activated even as he activates the other's potency and potentialities." Just as therapy with couples can help to resolve shared issues, so can individual issues be raised and addressed within this powerful, shared arena. Similarly, as couples have been in a relationship, individual issues will have been shared and blended into joint issues.

ORAL-SENSORY STAGE

In the first year of life, the ability to form nurturing relationships is important for the child's physical and psychological continuance. The crisis, in Erikson's (1963) theory, is the development of trust or mistrust. In addition, those who resolve this conflict successfully can develop hope.

For those who were abused, neglected, experienced significant loss, or who had inconsistent parenting, the development of trust may be difficult, and mistrust may be their basic stance. Rather than hope, the expectation of disappointment in relationships may be paramount. There is, however, the paradox of the opposite stance: unrealistic expectations, needs, and hopes are projected onto the other person. As these expectations crumble, the anger, disappointment, or mistrust, may alternately be placed on one's self or on the other.

It is important in working with a couple to understand the shared nature of these issues. Early in a relationship, a better functioning individual may experience difficulty with the mistrust of the partner, and these may be issues in counseling. If the relationship has existed for some time, however, it becomes important to understand why the seemingly better adjusted partner has elected to remain in this relationship, or how this partner has helped the issues to evolve.

Most commonly, the sources of a basic mistrust can be traced to early experiences for one or both partners, that have continued for much of their life. Where such factors exist for both partners, the relationship is replete with challenges and failed tests, and it becomes an arena in which the couple can continue to act out these conflicts.

Where these conflicts are visibly more present in one partner than the other, the other partner may need the ambivalent dependency of the first partner, or the feelings of righteousness or sacrifice from the unfounded suspicions and accusations. In the most serious of cases, other than those involving physical abuse in reaction to mistrust, one partner may psychologically torture the other by establishing unclear situations to exacerbate the mistrust, and, at least some of the time, prove a trustworthiness so that the other partner becomes unable even to trust mistrust, and may regress into stronger ambivalence and dependency.

As bleak as these situations sound, and they are difficult to resolve because of the primacy and continuing nature of these issues, as they are resolved they can provide powerful strengths, both individually and in the relationship. There are tremendous feelings of completeness, freedom, trust, and spontaneity. In one couple, the husband described the increasing understanding and resolution of these issues as "being free for the first time to love," while the wife described it as "being able to walk in the sunlight."

ANAL-MUSCULAR STAGE

During the second year of life, as the child gains control over the muscles of the body, independent muscular action becomes possible. Walking is an important component of this stage, as are the parental demands for toilet training. The child also begins to communicate verbally, and receives responses. The central developmental conflict is on autonomy vs. shame and doubt, and the successful resolution allows for the development of will.

It is difficult for most clients to retrieve more than fragments of memories from this period, particularly if events were not traumatic or unusual.

The most common themes brought to relationships revolve around an anxious uncertainty about oneself and the partner. The quality is generally not a suspiciousness of the partner, but a fear of one's self as not good enough, a failure, inadequate. Often, in the formative childhood years, one learned that he or she was not seen as adequate or capable, and independence should not be attempted: attempts were likely berated or sabotaged by parents.

In some cases, individuals with such backgrounds, particularly if they have come from abusive homes, will go on to find abusive relationships. Again, this paper cannot focus on abuse, but readers are directed to the excellent works of Walker (1986, 1984).

The general pattern is a fear of movement that requires the partner to be constantly encouraging, reassuring, and protective. While this may satisfy needs in some partners to be a guide and protector, this generally lasts only for the initial stages of the relationship. Over time the requirements become frustrating, draining, and burdensome. As the partner becomes angry or less responsive to the fearful dependency of the other, the fears, shame, and doubts likely will be exacerbated, creating even more intense demands, fueling a syndrome that likely will destroy the relationship.

Individuals coming into a relationship in which the battle for autonomy in earlier years was long-fought and problematic, can manifest a schizoid, counterdependent quality, making mutuality impossible to achieve. This partner may have an almost sadistic need to control the partner. Attempts by the partner to share and achieve mutuality will be perceived as entrapping threats to autonomy.

Where couples can confront these issues, a tremendous equalization and stability will develop over time in the relationship. At times the growing autonomy of a partner who moves away from shame and doubt may create a fear of loss in the other partner, who has been the stronger, reassuring individual. Where the relationship has involved genuine caring beyond the dependence, or such caring can develop, these issues can be worked through. There is an increasing sense of relief and joy in the relationship.

Where exaggerated autonomy has been the issue, there is a tremendous sense of tension reduction. One male client described it in different ways, in different sessions, "I don't always have to be wearing boxing gloves," and "a fortress wall is being taken down." His wife smilingly noted, "I can move toward him without feeling like I'm crossing a mine field . . . we can really touch."

As clients develop autonomy and will, there is sometimes a propulsion too rapidly to take charge or to make decisions. While most therapists do not insist clients make no decisions without prior consultation, therapists will walk an important line to support the client's and the couple's changes, while helping them examine the salient issues and forces, without frustrating moves toward autonomy.

PHALLIC-LOCOMOTOR STAGE

In the third to fifth or sixth years the critical developmental components for Freud revolved around the Oedipus/Electra conflicts. For Erikson, the broader psychosocial conflict centers around initiative vs. guilt, with the possibility of developing a sense of purpose following a successful resolution of these issues.

The child must be able to acknowledge and successfully integrate sexual and other impulses. The relationship with parents, and the attitudes of parents towards the experience and expression of impulses will be important. Beyond that, the child's ability to walk, talk, and think will be continually developing, fostering on-going interactions with people and the environment.

There are two general domains of unsuccessful outcomes, with concomitant relationship issues. Difficulties in acknowledging and integrating impulses, and problematic interpersonal relationships often reflect earlier, more traditionally labeled "neurotic" problems stemming from difficulties during this stage.

In this first pattern sexuality, in particular, is problematic. It is unenjoyable and threatening. The partner's demands may be acceded to out of guilt, or strategies may be employed to avoid sexual contact. Although not necessarily as rigid or compulsive as the pattern described in the previous section, the person in nonsexual spheres as well may opt for very conforming, conventional patterns, which the partner will come to find stifling.

As so often happens, the guilt and self-dislike of this pattern has a counterpart, generally known in extreme cases as the narcissistic or phallic-narcissistic character. Whether as a reaction-formation to guilt, or as a fixation at a time of self-indulgence, the individual is highly impulse-oriented. It must be noted that within appropriate limits such personality trends give us an exciting, spontaneous, and enjoyably expressive individual, who is well integrated and able to have meaningful relationships. As these trends become broader and more central personality structures, however, we find the person who can only take from others, and who uses them only as means to personal ends.

It is not surprising to find these two types in relationships together. The underlying similarities of their dynamics provides an unspoken, unconscious possibility for union, and in the differing overt personality styles a sort of balance may be achieved, at least temporarily.

Where these differing trends are only moderate personality components for each partner, it is possible to help them to understand each other, and to achieve an enjoyment of each other. Neither plays a dominant role in the relationship: rather, each takes a turn as the couple needs more outgoing or more intimate experiences.

In more severe cases, it is the overt differences and underlying similarities that may strongly draw the couple together, but that may also make a successful relationship more difficult. The more inhibited partner will feel overshadowed, inadequate, and guilty for relationship problems, while the more narcissistic will likely blame the partner for a perceived inability to change and the stifling quality of the relationship. After acting out, this individual may try to reform, but likely will relapse into impulsiveness, with guilt alternately accepted penitently and projected angrily. The ability of such couples to work profitably in therapy will depend not only on how pronounced and pervasive are these personality features, but also on the degree to which mutual loving and caring exist beyond these patterns.

Paul and Janice were an exceptionally attractive couple. He had a number of casual sexual relationships before marriage, but not in an exploitive sense. Paul enjoyed sharing sensual experiences, and was highly adventurous and spontaneous. This was reflected in his wanting to work in an outdoors, ranger-like setting after graduation. He had indulgent, loving parents, and as an only child who was exceptionally handsome, Paul was given much adoration and freedom.

Janice came from an affluent, religious family, with a father and mother who worked hard to move from the middle to the upper class. Janice and her parents placed less emphasis on enjoying the present as compared to planning for the future. Although popular in high school, she did not engage in sexual relations until she and Paul had dated for several weeks. She did not feel comfortable having premarital sex, but sensed it was important to Paul. Her goal for the future was for Paul to join her father's firm and become an executive with a good salary.

They had been married for two and a half years when they came into therapy. There were constant arguments about his career plans, his occasional use of marijuana and alcohol, and her unwillingness to engage playfully in sexual activities, or to join him in outdoor activities. Over the course of a year in therapy, their marital therapy went well, in the most disappointing sense: they recognized that they could not make the changes necessary to accommodate each other. The goal of therapy became a positive separation, without anger or bitterness. This was achieved. They continued to have strong feelings for each other, and over the next year continued to be friends and occasionally lovers. They were seen together in therapy during this period, and made great progress in understanding their needs and attraction to each other. Janice was the first to meet someone else, and while maintaining friendly ties with Paul, she withdrew from sexual contacts. Sometime later, he met a woman who shared his interests in the outdoors.

LATENCY

This is the longest of the pregenital stages, lasting from approximately age 5 or 6 until puberty. In Freudian thinking this reflects a relatively quiet time psychosexually, if all has gone well, with a consolidation of the pregenital patterns, a repression of the psychosexual issues, and the formation of the superego.

The psychosocial conflict for Erikson is industry vs. inferiority, with a sense of competence as the positive outcome. From Erikson's perspective, this is a critical period, not a quiet time. One leaves the home environment for the world of school and peers, and will find many areas in which to be valued or devalued. Within this context, children can learn to explore and express who they are and what they do. They may also learn to play roles to please others, and for some these roles become so fixed that later growth and development will be painful.

Younger individuals, still exploring their identity issues in their teens or early twenties, may be functioning around the roles learned in the latency period. The expression of related problems in a relationship is seen in "doing." The attempts are to please the partner by works or acts, not through a genuine personal relationship. For such individuals, there will be a feeling of at best treading water, and often sinking; trying to please in relationships, no matter how much one does, enough cannot be done, and so the person's self-perception is of never being good enough.

This pattern should not be confused with the so-called "workaholic." In this pattern described relative to the latency period production is geared to please the other and to reduce feelings of inferiority, but not to avoid the other.

Elaine and Jim had met when they both had successful careers and were in their late twenties. They married two years later. They had a caring relationship, and all had gone well while they dated. Elaine perceived Jim as a caring, sensitive, and attentive man and took the many things he did for her as an expression of his love. After they were married and living together, he seemed to be constantly focused on what he could do for her, needing continual reassurance that what he did was satisfactory. At first she assumed this was his reaction to being a newlywed. By the second year of marriage she was disturbed and concerned by the pervasiveness of his actions. What pleasure she derived from his attentiveness was fading.

Jim had come from a family where he was loved and respected, but he was also a quiet, shy, and small youngster. In school and with peers he was ignored, picked on, and ridiculed. When he was able to form friendships, he found himself feeling fearful and unworthy, and solicited approval and liking by being attentive to friends' needs, or any imagined need he perceived.

In the course of their therapy, Jim was able to grow and develop, and to achieve a meaningful sense of himself. His good parental situation, and his success later, had allowed him to develop well in other areas, such that his only problems were in friendships and intimate relationships. He and Elaine developed a very happy and mutual relationship in their marriage.

ADOLESCENCE

Erikson is perhaps best known for his work on this stage. He sees the central psychosocial conflict as identity vs. confusion, with fidelity as the outcome strength of this stage.

Identity encompasses many spheres, including sexuality, vocational developments, a temporal orientation, and other domains (Erikson, 1968). It is not, when achieved, a final statement of "I am this and that," but rather a sense of present but changing continuity. When this continuity is absent there is a confusion about the self, and the present has a threatening, expansive quality, while the past feels disconnected and the future remains a distant abstraction.

For adolescents the struggle for identity involves considerable anxiety, confusion, and experimentation. Those who do not successfully resolve these struggles during this stage will likely be confronted by them again later in life. These struggles will strongly affect an individual's ability to enter into and maintain relationships. As will be discussed, there are likely to be related issues for both individuals, and these not only will affect the relationship, but likely will considerably shape the direction of therapy as well.

In the successful resolution, identity achievement, the adolescent develops a flexible sense of self that provides continuity in the present, but that also will grow and change as needed with continuing life situations. As the individual feels whole and with a direction, fidelity to one's self and others is possible.

Other outcomes can also occur. Many individuals will only partially, and perhaps not at all, achieve a sense of identity, and will proceed into adulthood with continuing identity confusion. This confusion may be mild or severe. In the latter cases, Erikson (1988) notes it may appear to be, though is not psychotic in nature.

Identity foreclosure is another resolution possible. Rather than confront the troubling uncertainties of the search for identity, sometimes in conjunction with familial or peer pressure, an individual accepts a set of values without any real questioning. Much like a shell, the foreclosed identity may protect the individual, but it can become constraining and stultifying. As natural tendencies for growth and change develop, and external situations demand adaptation, threat and conflict can again emerge, particularly if the resulting stressors cause the shell to break too quickly. Sometimes in therapy, as the foreclosure begins to dissolve, the individual will complain of having been happier, in a way, before therapy.

A negative identity provides yet another solution to these conflicts. When an individual cannot develop a sense of self embracing more conventionally accepted values and roles, an identity based on the values of a socially rejected system becomes an alternative. This allows the individual entrance and acceptance into groups with similar negative values. Religious cults, "bikers," "skinheads," and drug-oriented groups are some contemporary examples.

Although any combination of these identity patterns is possible within couples, it is this writer's experience that individuals tend to form relationships with others roughly comparable in identity issues. This is partly a selection process, and partly based on the ability to endure beyond the early stages of acquaintanceship required for a relationship. Foreclosed individuals generally need others with similar systems in order to maintain the foreclosure. Individuals with negative identities risk challenging the only ways in which they feel positive about themselves if they are in relationships with more positively identity achieved individuals. An identity confused person cannot typically provide the stability and fidelity an achieved person would need. Confused individuals, however, can justify their own confusion through that of another, in the sense of a mutual projection of blame for problems, and a system that may allow for "openness" as a guise for confusion.

The most common of the pairings of individuals coming to therapy with different identity issues has been the confused individual with a foreclosed individual. The foreclosed individual's certainties provide an anchor for the confused individual. Often there are mutual dependency needs involved, with the confused partner being overtly more dependent, and the foreclosed individual requiring this symbiotic dependency. Movement by the confused individual to a more satisfactory identity achievement position will be quite threatening to the system and the partner.

Therapists working with adolescent couples, or perhaps young adult couples still dealing with these issues, have an advantage in that these issues, as well as the residual issues from other stages of childhood, are close to the surface, often readily experienced and quite visible to the therapist. There are distinct disadvantages as well. The issues may, in fact, be too close to the surface for the adolescent to acknowledge. Perhaps more commonly, the adolescent couple may not have the maturity and experience with which to recognize and deal with the issues. Similarly, they may not have yet repeated these patterns often enough to recognize their intractably pernicious effects on the relationship. All too often adolescents resort to magical thinking about relationships, with expectations that "love will conquer all," or "things will work themselves out," without any understanding of the issues involved.

It would be too lengthy to illustrate all of the possible patterns with cases. Assuming that couples come in with relatively equal identity issues, except as previously noted, a brief summary of relationship issues is possible. Foreclosed individuals likely will have had a mutually protective system that has become stultifying, or is threatened by the identity movement of one partner. The love, acceptance, and caring for the other will have to transcend issues of narrowness and dogmatism not unlike those discussed by Rokeach (1960).

Negative identities function somewhat like foreclosed identities. As one moves toward more conventional values, the other will have to allow the space with which to explore other possibilities, without being threatened. Where negative identities have been developed for strong self-defensive issues, this can be quite difficult.

For identity confused couples, the ability to sort out issues, and to develop purpose and meaning will be incredibly liberating. Unfortunately, as some individuals come to develop a sense of self, they may grow apart. This is not necessarily the case, but when it occurs it will require the therapist to help them separate in a positive way. In other cases, of course, the couple will develop newer and stronger senses of meaning from the relationship and their commitment to each other.

Finally, it should be noted that the identity issues may emerge at any time during life, if a foreclosed, confused, or negative system has been maintained. Quite often when so-called "midlife crisis" issues affect relationships, we are encountering identity issues that have been sealed up, but that have finally broken through.

YOUNG ADULTHOOD

The previously discussed developmental issues are often seen in therapy with couples around the crisis of this stage, intimacy vs. isolation. Love, meaningful interdependent sharing, both at sexual and emotional levels, is the outcome strength of this stage.

If individuals have progressed satisfactorily through the previous stages, then this stage will be easier. It will not be magic, or simple. Individuals likely will need to explore a variety of relationships with different people. Such exploration, however, will not be exploitive, and often where a lasting romantic relationship does not develop, or does not continue, a friendship can. As would be expected, individuals able to achieve such good relationships, or to deal with the issues of this stage, are typically not seen in therapy. As Erikson (1963, p. 264) notes, "the danger of this stage is that intimate, competitive, and combative relations are experienced with and against the same people," with individuals establishing "isolation a deux" (Erikson, 1963, p. 266).

In working with couples where intimacy is problematic, the different kinds of intimacies, and levels of intimacies must be recognized. In many cases, at the point of entrance into therapy, emotional intimacy, both at deeper and more casual levels will be difficult, and sexual intimacy may be problematic as well. For other couples, one will encounter the statement, "In bed, the sex is fine. It's out of bed we have problems." Intimacy, in the sense of a meaningful relationship with the possibility of both true and realistic love, will take some time to establish. Some individuals may mistake infatuation for this, or may search for the "perfect" person, and hence remain isolated.

More commonly, where intimacy is a problem, an "as-if" relationship may be created. The couple establishes roles which they act out meticulously to maintain the appearance of a meaningful relationship. Of course, at deeper levels they will recognize this play-acting, and resent it, or feel some emptiness. Other couples will create a "pseudointimacy," by sharing many things, but never really themselves. Exotic trips or experiences, or the use of drugs, may facilitate the sense of pseudointimacy. Another common marker relating to these issues are feelings of hurt, anger, and jealousy over non-sexual but emotionally intimate relationships one partner may have with friends.

With younger couples, many of the issues from past stages will be more clearly visible. As we move toward a society with individuals marrying later, involvement with career and less intimate relationships may allow for the submerging of these issues until they are forced to the surface in the context of a potentially intimate and lasting relationship. As people learn to live alone, it may be more difficult to return to the arena of relationships and deal with these painful and threatening issues.

Naturally, in the course of working with individuals and couples having problems at this stage, one needs to examine other developmental issues, as described previously, that may be manifesting themselves through intimacy issues. In many cases, painful issues from the past will inhibit one or both partners' attempts to establish true intimacy and mutuality. The issues of intimacy, and the related conflicts, involving more current issues also must be examined.

Lee, a successful 30 year old car salesman met and fell in love with Anne, a 28 year old college professor. Both had seemingly good levels of adjustment, with no major crises in their lives.They had good parental histories, and relationships with peers.Each had meaningful, but not lasting relationships until they met each other. Both had recognized some unwillingness earlier in their lives to sacrifice career development for relationships, and felt that they had perhaps put such issues on a "back burner."

For Lee, his initial months in the relationship were exhilarating: he had never had a person he felt as close with, nor had any of his sexual relationships been as meaningful. Anne felt she had found the person she could share her life with. Yet in the second six months of their relationship fights began to emerge over the smallest things. As we explored the issues in therapy, each felt a sense of loss of freedom in the commitment to each other, and there were uncertainties about this. Lee had become anxious about how much he "needed" Anne. She was "angry with him" because she devoted less time to her research and writing.

Therapy required both of them to examine their attitudes and feelings about relationships in general, and particularly about each other. Over time, the depth of their caring matured, and they were able to resolve the issues, marry, and have a mutually-enhancing relationship.

MIDDLE AGE

The crisis here is generativity vs. stagnation, a sense that one is contributing to the world in some meaningful way, or that one has accomplished nothing. The outcome strength of this stage is care.

In many cases, couples coming to therapy at this stage will reflect issues with identity or intimacy that have surfaced due either to dissatisfaction that has accumulated, or to stage-related changes that will have reactivated these issues. For other couples, of course, unique stage-related events will activate a crisis of generativity, and affect the relationship by the input of these issues, and perhaps by calling the relationship itself into question.

Therapists will have seen such issues in the sense of loss experienced with the recognition of the loss of youth, or the loss of career mobility. Dreams will not have been recognized. The family, with the children having grown, will no longer be a focus for the partners. Individuals, over the years, may have grown in different directions, and now the relationship has become hollow. From an important different direction, due to conflicts around generativity, one partner may blame the other and/or the relationship for a more personal sense of hollowness or meaninglessness.

In therapy, the couple must examine not only their history and assumptions about the relationship, but their commitment to restoring or creating new meaning for the relationship. If the foundations for the relationship have been good, and the issues are more stage-related, the likelihood of a better relationship emerging after therapy is quite good. Where other, more long-lasting issues have finally surfaced, the possibilities become more problematic. Much will depend on how much the couple can come to resolve these long-standing issues, and develop the intimacy and meaning necessary for a good relationship.

At the same time, a relationship thrown into crisis because of generativity-related conflicts can use these for an examination of issues that will allow for a new power and direction in a relationship that may have become more routine than meaningful. Therapists who have had such outcomes with couples will note how often they seem like mature newlyweds!

OLD AGE

The last of the stages, the crisis here is integrity vs. despair, with wisdom as the positive outcome. The crisis forces individuals and couples to assess life, for a determination of how worthwhile it has been.

It is the consensus of therapists with whom I have discussed this stage that it is rare to see a couple at this stage of life in therapy, barring unusual physical or psychological changes affecting the relationship. Problem patterns likely will have been accepted as part of life, or resolved. Perhaps the one exception occurs when a spouse, generally the husband, retires, and the couple is forced to spend more time together than before, with new strains added, or perhaps submerged ones reactivated.

Too often have therapists minimized the issues, or possibilities for change in older clients (King, 1974). Similarly, the absence of clients at this stage may change with the "greying of the Baby Boomers," and our extended longevity. As couples end their careers and retire together, or form new relationships after divorce or the death of a spouse, increasing numbers of couples at this stage may enter therapy.

While limited data is available on therapy with couples at such stages, depression and frustration with aging, with the partner's demands, and with a sense of lost opportunities, seem most to affect the relationship. At this stage, as at all stages, the possibilities for meaningful communication and sharing have the power not only to revitalize the relationship but also to help each partner find their sense of integrity. Certainly more work is needed on the issues and possibilities with this age group.

CONCLUDING COMMENTS

It is hoped that this paper will provide therapists with other ways of understanding the issues couples may bring to therapy. The conflict(s) seen in a couple's relationship may in fact reflect not only developmental issues of one partner, but issues that become systemic in the relationship. Erikson's theories provide a useful vehicle by which to understand these developmental issues, to facilitate their exploration in therapy, and to allow them to become sources of strength and growth for the couple as well as for each partner individually. Although one might argue that issues may be more specific to one partner or the other, after a relationship has existed for even a modest length of time, the issues will in some way become shared. Often each individual's issues will interact with those of the partner, producing shared issues around these developmental themes.

Where couples come to a relationship disillusioned with each other, and likely with themselves, it is important to realize the sources of the disillusioning process: for to be disillusioned means not that one began realistically, but that one began with illusion. So often these illusions reflect problematic developmental themes, that had no possibility of resolution. The anger, bitterness, hostility, and related emotions can be defused, and paths found, for the individual and the couple, that will be mutually fulfilling for the individuals and the couple as a unit. As these are understood and integrated, and as positive developments within the relationship are created, the therapeutic process works its healing course.

NOTE

1. All references to the components of the eight life cycle stages proposed by Erikson are based on Erikson (1963) unless otherwise noted.

REFERENCES

Erikson, E. H. (1963) *Childhood and society* (second edition). New York: Norton.
Erikson, E. H. (1964) *Insight and responsibility*. New York: Norton.
Erikson, E. H. (1968) *Identity: youth and crisis*. New York: Norton.
Evans, R. I. (1981) *Dialogue with Erik Erikson*. New York: Praeger.
King, P. H. M. (1974) Notes on the psychoanalysis of older patients. *Journal of Analytical Psychology, 19*, 22-37.
Rokeach, M (1960) *The open and closed mind*. New York: Basic Books.
Smelser, N. J. (1980) Issues in the study of love and adulthood. In N. J. Smelser & E. H. Erikson (Eds.) *Themes of work and love in adulthood*. Cambridge, MA: Harvard University Press.
Walker, L. E. A. (1984) *The battered woman syndrome*. New York: Springer.
Walker, L. E. A. (1986) Assessment and intervention with battered women. In P. A. Keller and S. R. Heyman (Eds.) *Innovations in clinical practice, volume 6*. Sarasota, FL: Professional Resource Exchange.

Suitable for Reframing:
The Myers-Briggs Type Indicator
in Couples Therapy

George Atkinson, Jr.

SUMMARY. Reframing is a therapeutic technique used by therapist to redefine or relabel a couple's perceived reality surrounding dysfunctional interactions. Reframing helps the couple reorganize their understanding of those interactions in ways that free them to utilize personal resources for constructive change. The Myers-Briggs Type Indicator (MBTI) is uniquely suited to the process and goals of reframing. With its underlying positive regard for human nature, the MBTI becomes a convenient tool for helping couples discover that individual differences do not have to be barriers to intimacy, but can be reliable assets when viewed from the proper perspective.

Individual differences that have the potential of inhibiting or destroying intimacy, exist within the personalities of practically every couple. Couples often have differing preferences, perspectives, opinions, beliefs, and expectations that may disrupt and confound the functional harmony of the relationship.

Relationship partners may have different capacities for emotional expressiveness (Dosser, Balswick, & Halverson, 1983); variable abilities to send and receive verbal and nonverbal messages (Noller, 1980, 1981; Hall, 1979); different levels of decision-making skills (Stuart, 1980); unequal problem-solving skills (Jacobson & Margolin, 1979); different aptitudes for expressing praise, appreciation, and empathy (Warren & Gilner, 1978); and differing sexual needs (Hei-

George Atkinson, Jr., PhD, is Counseling Psychologist at the Counseling Center of Clemson University, South Palmetto Blvd., Clemson, SC 29634-4022.

man, Gladue, Roberts & LoPiccolo, 1986). Individual differences may precipitate struggles over power and control (Haley, 1963; Madanes, 1981), sex role conflicts (Margolin, Talovic, Fernandez, & Onoratro, 1983), violence (Minuchin, 1984; Cook, & Frantz-Cook, 1984), coercive interactions (Piercy, 1983), and conflicts with the family of origin (Framo, 1981; Kerr, 1985). Many problems arise over how personal differences are integrated into the economy of the relationship (Karpel & Strauss, 1983). Couples slip into patterns of recurrent and destructive interactions from which they are unable to escape because they fail to comprehend, or even imagine, an alternative solution or reality.

REFRAMING

An effective therapeutic tool for opening up new behavioral options for couples is the technique referred to by Watzlawick, Weakland, and Fisch (1974, p. 92) as "the gentle art of reframing." Reframing means redefining or relabeling a perceived reality to create a slightly different and more constructive perspective (Sauber, L'Abate, and Weeks, 1985). Reframing changes a negative into a positive by altering the conceptual frame of reference in which a situation is embedded and evaluated, in order to change the meaning of the event without changing the facts (Sherman & Fredman, 1986). When reframing is successful, couples attribute new meanings to their behaviors and view each other more positively (Constantine, Fish, & Piercy, 1984).

Because it presents the couple with a new "map of the world" (Elkaim, 1986) by which to orient their entrenched and counterproductive perceptions, reframing can exert tremendous therapeutic power in clinical situations. Reframing impasses in therapy accomplishes several desirable outcomes for both the therapist and the client. It assists the therapist in managing the interview process by: (a) eliminating resistance by positively relabeling identified motives, needs, desires, and intentions of both past and present negative behaviors (Lankton & Lankton, 1983, p. 338); (b) increasing therapist influence in joining the relationship system (Minuchin, 1974); and (c) maneuvering hesitant clients into committing to the therapeutic process

(Bergman, 1985, p. 44). Reframing benefits the clients by: (a) engendering hope, optimism, and even excitement in couples as they approach the task of reconstituting their relationship (Sherman & Fredman, 1986); (b) infusing new purpose and determination into the couple's search for a better understanding of each other (Sherman & Fredman, 1986, p. 199); (c) preventing either partner from assuming the role of villain; (d) affirming and validating the messages of both partners' equal respect (Lankton & Lankton, 1983, p. 15); (e) redirecting couples away from the usual downward spiral of relationships caught in self-perpetuating cycles of negative interactions (Sherman & Fredman, 1986, p. 200); (f) engendering new energy to find more effective methods of satisfying the individual's actual needs (Lankton & Lankton, 1983, p. 336); and (g) readying the couple for new and desirable learning experiences by questioning the perceptions of old problematic thoughts, feelings, and behavior patterns.

Couples most readily adopt a reframed perspective when it is offered to them in terms consistent with the way that they view their world (Bergman, 1985, p. 44). Reframes not congenial with familiar categories risk falling victim to the couple's natural resistance to change. By allowing for the couple's views, expectations, premises, and assumptions, the successful reframer helps the troubled partners move from a divergent to a therapeutically consistent belief system (Lankton & Lankton, 1983, p. 338).

Because timing is often the difference between a reframe's acceptance or rejection, Kantor (1985, p. 31) suggests attempting to reframe only after (a) gaining a profound grasp of each individual's explanation of the situation and his or her role in it, (b) gathering a solid base concerning the dynamics of the system and how each partner views the other's contribution, and (c) making very strong and concrete joining moves to establish rapport with the couple. It is important for the clinician to remember that reframing, like any other intervention, must occur within a completely ethical framework and should be employed congruently and sincerely by the therapist or not at all (Lankton & Lankton, 1983, p. 338). A reframe should not be concocted out of thin air. It probably will not generate the necessary therapeutic power for change if the intervention does not ring true for the couple (Bergman, 1985, p. 44).

MYERS-BRIGGS TYPE INDICATOR

Type Theory

The instrument is based on C.G. Jung's theory of psychological type. Type theory provides therapists and couples with a convenient conceptual framework for understanding diversity in human personality. It allows people to view individual differences in a positive and constructive manner. Jung (1923) believed apparently random behavior in people could be explained if there was a greater understanding of how individuals prefer to use their mental processes of perception and judgment. A person becomes aware of things, places, events, and ideas in the environment through the process of perception. An individual reaches conclusions and decisions about what is perceived through the process of judgment. While each person uses both of these mental processes, Jung postulated that each individual has a natural tendency to prefer one over the other in the same way each person has a preference for choosing to write with the right or left hand.

Jung describes two distinct ways of perceiving. One is *sensing* (S), by which one achieves awareness directly through the senses, and the other is *intuition* (N), by which one becomes aware of ideas or associations indirectly, as expressed in hunches or "impressions." Similarly, there are two contrasting ways of using judgment or making decisions. Using *thinking* (T) judgment, the decision maker follows a logical, analytic process aimed at an impersonal finding. Using *feeling* (F) judgment, the decision maker follows an equally rational process in which personal conviction and subjective values are the most important criteria.

Interest in the inner and outer worlds also governs how people use perception and judgment. According to Jung's (1923) concepts of *extraversion* (E) and *introversion* (I), an extravert focuses on the outer world of people and things, while introverts give their main attention to the inner world of concepts and ideas. Isabel Briggs Myers, one of the MBTI's developers, added one more preference to help distinguish and understand type–the choice between the *judging* (J) attitude and the *perceptive* (P) attitude as a method for managing the outer world (Myers & McCaulley, 1985). Those who prefer the judging life-style choose order and structure in dealing with the world. Those who prefer the perceptive life-style value flexibility and spontaneity. Individuals choose either perception or judgment as a dominant mode to guide their lives and the other as a secondary, assisting process.

People define their psychological type through the exercise of their individual preferences. The combination of choices on the four dimensions yields a possibility of 16 different types. Each type has its unique strengths, and each person's personality can be framed in a positive light.

Administration and Verification

The therapist follows the usual professional and ethical conventions of good testing when administering the Myers-Briggs Type Indicator (MBTI) for reframing purposes. Specific instructions are clearly explained in the manual (Myers & McCaulley, 1985). Particular points to emphasize are: (1) the MBTI is an indicator and not a test, (2) there are no wrong answers just as there are no good or bad types, and (3) all types are considered valuable, having their own strengths and weaknesses. Regardless of the type, each individual uses both sides of the preferences; but as with handedness, each uses most the preferences with which he or she is the more adept.

Once the indicator is scored and the couple's individual types known, the clinician can then begin to redefine the dysfunctional interactions and begin to nudge the couple out of what Minuchin and Fishman (1981, p. 76) call their "homeostatic stubbornness." During the verification process, described in detail by Myers and McCaulley (1985), the individual identifies and owns his or her type description. While introducing the concepts and vocabulary of type, the therapist may initiate preliminary reframing moves. As the verification process continues, the clients usually experience a certain amount of confusion as they attempt to understand the new ideas. This is expected and even useful in securing the client's cooperation and in dissipating resistance (Erickson, 1964). Each partner in the dyad should understand that the power to confirm or disconfirm the results resides with him or her, and the therapist should solicit reactions to the results. Becoming a participant in the verification process, the client accepts and owns the results more readily, and, therefore, becomes more open to the reframer's suggestions.

Several publications [i.e., *Introduction to Type* (Myers, 1980) and *Looking at Type* (Page, 1983)] are available to assist in explaining MBTI results. These not only facilitate an understanding of the concepts, but also augment the credibility of the instrument. Increased credibility enhances acceptance of the reframed perspective. While some couples will need convincing, many will receive the results willingly, even eagerly, because it is information presented by an "expert" and based on a "test" (Goldman, 1971, p. 346). It is important, therefore, that the therapist make careful and judicious use of the clients' openness without exploiting their confidence in the therapeutic process.

Indicator Characteristics

The MBTI (Form G) has 126 items in a forced choice format and usually takes about 35 minutes to complete. It can be scored by hand or computer. Software for on-site scoring is available from Consulting Psychologists Press, Inc. (CPP). Computerized reports are also available from CPP and The Center for the Application of Psychological Type using Form G and the much longer Form J, including a relationship report expressly for couples (Hammer, 1987). Myers and McCaulley (1985) report favorable reliability data. Split-half internal consistency coefficients for the four dimensions range from .82 to .86 (M = .84). Internal consistency coefficients based on coefficient alpha range from .80 to .83 (M = .81). Stability coefficients range from .80 to .87 (M = .85) after 7-week interval, and range from .45 to .58 (M = .51) after a 4-year interval.

UNIQUENESS OF FIT

The MBTI is a unique and convenient instrument for reframing in couples therapy because its underlying theory and assumptions are resonant with the goals of reframing. Since the MBTI is not pathology-based, it lends itself to ascribing positive connotations to what is perceived by the couple as problems behaviors (Selvini Palazzoli, Boscolo, Cecchin, & Prata, 1974).

Since all of the sixteen types are legitimate styles of living, each individual, and his or her viewpoint, is given respect. This assists the couple in avoiding the bitter cycle of blame and recrimination. Because no type is worse or better than another, differences can be reframed as assets to appreciate and to utilize for mutual advantage. They are not necessarily divisive barriers, but can become bridges to mutual understanding and support. The MBTI offers the couple a completely different explanation for their behavior by recasting negatively inferred motives, intentions, desires, and needs in a new and benevolent light.

Rubin (1976) reports couples often have problems because they lack a shared language. Using the terminology of type as a *lingua franca*, the therapist can teach the couple a language they can share, and use in discovering alternative means of satisfying their needs. Once their difficulties have been defined in terms of the MBTI, the couple will be less able to completely return to their old views and perceptions.

Couples frequently begin spontaneously applying type concepts to their current situation. Since clients often seem to have a natural inclination to accept uncritically the results about themselves based on an inventory or test (Goldman, 1971), the therapist can tap this natural credulity to enhance the validity of reframes. The basically optimistic view of human nature promoted by the MBTI enables the therapist to communicate optimism and hope to couples who, by the time they reach the counselor's office, have essentially abandoned the belief that a solution exists to their misery.

CASE ILLUSTRATION

Bob, 41, and Beth, 39, have been married for eighteen years and have two children. He is a manager in a small manufacturing company, while she is an elementary school teacher. They have an active social life centered mainly around his business associates and contacts. The couple entered therapy at Beth's insistence. Bob agreed only after learning his wife had retained a divorce lawyer. Beth said that she "couldn't take it anymore." Bob said he did not know what the trouble was and thought that "things were just fine."

Beth felt they had problems in several areas of their marriage, but her overriding concern was the continuous stream of criticism she received from Bob. The therapist observed that Bob did appear to have a caustic wit and a sarcastic way of pointing out whatever displeased him. He usually couched these comments in what he considered to be humor, but that did nothing to reduce the sting of his remarks until Beth finally believed she "could do nothing right." Even when confronted with some of the statements he made to his wife in therapy and with the effect they had on her, Bob responded by saying that his wife "had always been too emotional and taken such things too seriously."

The MBTI was administered after the first session and the third session was used for the verification process. Bob decided the description of ESTJ fit him, and Beth confirmed ENFJ was best for her. Both Bob and Beth, the therapist explained, shared the attitude of *extraversion* (E). They both enjoyed an active social life together and apart. Since they both also preferred *judgment* (J), Bob and Beth tended to lead organized lives. The problem appeared to be in the differences they had in gathering and processing information from the world. Since Bob is an ST, he tended to lean toward practical matter-of-factness and impersonal analysis of the facts before him and, being a T, had a strong sensibility toward "truth" and "the right way of doing things," i.e., his way. However, Beth, being an NF, was more sensitive to people, valued personal warmth, feelings, and understanding, and was adept in communicating with most people. Beth saw Bob's remarks as personal attacks on her competence and worth as an individual. Bob thought his comments at home were just like the ones he made at the office and were not intended to be taken personally. He was just trying to "straighten things out."

Using the MBTI as a starting point, the therapist reframed the destructive interaction by putting it in a more positive context. He explained that the heart of their problem seemed to be one of caring for each other too much and wanting to protect each other. Thus, Beth was not the overly emotional female Bob thought she was. She was someone who experienced deeply her feelings and values, and cared openly about those of others as indicated by the dominant F in her type. When she would react to what she saw as criticism of her or the children by telling them that their father really did not mean it or by becoming withdrawn and distant, she was really protecting him from discovering how much emotional damage he was doing to the whole family. However misguided the strategy seemed now, it was done in Bob's best interest. Beth, at this point, began to cry quietly and nod her head affirmatively.

On the other hand, the therapist explained that Bob was not the acid-tongued ogre she suspected. Bob took no delight in being harsh and critical. Instead, he had a passion for truth and for seeing things always handled in the correct manner. His desire was really to share with his wife and family the benefits of his considerable experience in management and life. By insisting on having things done his way, Bob thought he was sparing Beth the future difficulties and inconveniences of having to remedy jobs improperly done. Bob concurred with this assessment. His criticisms were not meant as personal attacks, but as loving assistance. He had not realized how painful these attempts at offering help had been for his wife. He did not really understand her reactions, but he was willing to search for new ways to offer help and to make a greater effort to understand his wife's and his children's "truth."

Beth began to feel differently about Bob as she considered his criticisms merely fumbling attempts to offer assistance, rather than harshly critical and deliberately acrimonious remarks. She was willing to give the relationship another try, even when warned that things might not improve right away. Bob responded that he had a new respect for his wife's feelings and a desire to learn how to talk to her without causing her so much pain. Bob and Beth still had problems to work through, but they regained their will to try to resolve them with renewed hope and enthusiasm after the therapist reframed their destructive interactions using the MBTI.

Bob and Beth had a number of problems to work on in subsequent weeks. Their therapy moved into deeper divisions in their relationship and progress was steady, if slow. While not all behaviors in a couple's relationship are amenable to positive reframing, the MBTI proved in this instance to be an effective supplement to their overall therapy as a couple by assisting them to begin to move past intransigent patterns of destructive interactions. It also provided the couple and the therapist with a positive theme to which they could return when other impasses became obvious.

CONCLUSION

Reframing is a therapeutic technique useful in helping couples redefine, reorganize, and/or relabel a perceived reality. This often involves putting a positive connotation on negatively considered interactions. This positive relabeling may allow them to utilize their personal resources for constructive change. The underlying theory and positive focus of the MBTI make it an ideal instrument to employ in reframing the destructive interactions of couples which often result from differing personal preferences, perceptions, expectations, and beliefs. The reframing goals of reducing resistance and changing the focus of the struggling individuals are entirely compatible with the developmental emphasis of the MBTI. The instrument makes an excellent reframing tool because it allows marital partners to view each other, and the relationship, in distinctly different and more positive terms. This frees them to attempt new and more adaptive methods of interacting.

REFERENCES

Bergman, J. S. (1985). *Fishing for barracuda: Pragmatics of brief systemic therapy.* New York: Norton & Co.

Constantine, J. A., Fish, L. S., & Piercy, F. P. (1984). A systematic procedure for teaching positive connotation. *Journal of Marital and Family Therapy, 10*(3), 313-315.

Cook, D. R., & Frantz-Cook, A. (1984). A systematic treatment approach to wife battering. *Journal of Marital and Family Therapy, 10*(1), 83-94.

Dossier, D. A., Jr., Balswick, J. O., & Halverson, Jr. (1983). Situational context of emotional expressiveness. *Journal of Counseling Psychology, 30,* 375-387.

Elkaim, M. (1986). A systematic approach to couple therapy. *Family Process, 25*(1), 35-42.

Erickson, M. H. (1964). The confusion technique in hypnosis. *The American Journal of Clinical Hypnosis, 6,* 183-207.

Framo, J. L. (1981). The integration of marital therapy with sessions with family of origin. In A. S. Gurman & D. P. Kniskern (Eds.), *Handbook of Family Therapy* (pp. 133-158). New York: Brunner/Mazel.

Goldman, L. (1971). *Using tests in counseling.* New York: Appleton-Century-Crofts.

Haley, J. (1963). *Strategies of psychotherapy.* New York: Grune & Stratton.

Hall, J. (1979). Gender, gender roles, and nonverbal communication skills. In R.

Rosenthal (Ed.), *Skill in nonverbal communication: Individual differences* (pp. 32-67). Cambridge, MA: Oelgeschlager, Gunn, & Hain.

Hammer, A. L. (1987). *MBTI relationship report: Manual.* Palo Alto, CA: Consulting Psychologist Press.

Heiman, J. R., Gladue, B. A., Roberts, C. W., & LoPiccolo, J. (1986). Historical and current factors discriminating sexually functional from sexually dysfunctional married couples. *Journal of Marital and Family Therapy, 12*(2), 163-174.

Jacobsen, N. S., & Margolin, G. (1979). *Marital therapy: Strategies based on social learning and behavior exchange principles.* New York: Brunner/Mazel.

Jung, C. G. (1923). *Psychological types.* New York: Harcourt, Brace.

Kantor, D. (1985). Couples therapy, crisis induction, and change. In A. S. Gurman (Ed.), *Casebook of marital therapy.* New York: Guilford Press.

Karpel, M. A., & Strauss, E. S. (1983). *Family evaluation.* New York: Gardner Press.

Kerr, M. E. (1985). Obstacles to differentiation of self. In A. S. Gurman (Ed.), *Casebook of Marital Therapy* (pp. 111-154). New York: Guilford Press.

Lankton, S. R., & Lankton, C. H. (1983). *The answer within: A clinical framework of Ericksonian hypnotherapy.* New York: Brunner/Mazel.

Madanes, C. (1981). *Strategic family therapy.* San Francisco: Jossey-Bass.

Margolin, G., Talovic, S., Fernandez, V., & Onorato, R. (1983). Sex role considerations and behavioral marital therapy: Equal does not mean identical. *Journal of Marital and Family Therapy, 9*(20), 131-146.

Minuchin, S. (1974). *Families and family therapy.* Cambridge: Harvard University Press.

Minuchin, S (1984). *Family kaleidoscope: Images of violence and healing.* Cambridge, MA: Harvard University Press.

Minuchin, S., & Fishman, H. C. (1981). *Family therapy techniques.* Cambridge, MA: Harvard University Press.

Myers, I. B. (1980). *Introduction to Type.* Palo Alto, CA: Consulting Psychologists Press.

Myers, I. B., & McCaulley, M. H. (1985). *Manual: A guide to the development and use of the Myers-Briggs Type Indicator.* Palo Alto, CA: Consulting Psychologist Press.

Noller, P. (1980). Misunderstanding in marital communication: A study of couples' nonverbal communication. *Journal of Personality and Social Psychology, 41,* 272-278.

Noller, P. (1981). Gender and marital adjustment level differences in decoding messages from spouses and strangers. *Journal of Personality and Social Psychology, 39,* 1135-1148.

Page, E. C. (1983). *Looking at type.* Gainesville, FL: Center for the Application of Psychological Type.

Piercy, F. P. (1983). A game for interrupting coercive marital interaction. *Journal of Marital and Family Therapy, 9*(4), 435.

Rubin, L.B. (1976). *Worlds of pain: Life in the working-class family.* New York: Basic Books.

Sauber, S.R., L'Abate, L., & Weeks, G. R. (1985). *Family therapy: Basic concepts and terms*. Rockville, MD: Aspen.

Selvini Palazzoli, M., Boscolo, L., Cecchin, G. & Prata, G. (1978). *Paradox and counterparadox*. New York; Jason Aronson.

Sherman, R., & Fredman, N. (1986). *Handbook of structured techniques in marriage and family therapy*. New York: Brunner/Mazel.

Stuart, R. B. (1980). *Helping couples change: A social learning approach to marital therapy*. New York: Guilford Press.

Warren, N. J., & Gilner, F. H. (1978). Measurement of positive assertive behaviors: The behavioral test of tenderness expression. *Behavior Therapy, 9*, 178-184.

Watzlawick, P., Weakland, J. H., & Fisch, R. (1974). *Change: Principles of problem formation and problem resolution*. New York: Norton & Co.

Differentiation of Self and Marital Adjustment of Clinical and Nonclinical Spouses

Gilbert J. Greene
Tamara Feigal Mabee

SUMMARY. Bowen theory posits that spouses in problematic marriages are lower on differentiation of self and marital adjustment than spouses in nonproblematic marriages. This paper reports the findings from an empirical study which provide support for this aspect of Bowen theory. Differentiation of self and marital adjustment were also found to be moderately, positively related to each other. Implications for clinical practice and research are discussed.

One factor mentioned in the literature that contributes to marital adjustment is the level of differentiation of self of spouses (Bowen, 1978). While much has been written in the areas of differentiation of self and marital adjustment, no research has been done which examines clinical and nonclinical populations on these two variables. This paper reports results of a study which compared the differences between spouses in marital therapy and spouses who have never been in marital therapy on the dimensions of marital adjustment and differentiation of self.

Bowen (1978) called differentiation of self the cornerstone of his Family Theory. According to Kear (1978), differentiation of self, as defined by Bowen is "the process by which a person begins to mature emotionally and individuates from his[her] family of origin, at the same time separating the thinking and feeling aspects of his[her]

Gilbert J. Greene, PhD, ACSW, is Associate Professor at Ohio State University, College of Social Work, 1947 College Road, Columbus, OH 43210.
Tamara Feigal Mabee, MSW, is in private practice in St. Cloud, MN 56301.

personality" (p. 14). Bowen conceptualized differentiation of self as a continuum from low to high.

Those people with high levels of differentiation of self are able to distinguish feeling from fact and behave accordingly. High level people are regularly involved with their families of origin but are able to relate to family members in a flexible manner. People with high levels of differentiation of self are able to cope successfully with a broad range of life situations. High level people are able to cope with stressful situations as well as with emotional intimacy with another person or times when they are alone.

People who are low on differentiation of self are greatly affected and motivated by feelings. They have difficulty separating feeling from fact and are extremely attached to their family of origin. Those at the lower end of the differentiation of self continuum are not as adaptable to stress and are emotionally dependent on others. People such as this are consistently emotionally reactive to stressful situations and a major motivating factor is the immediate reduction of anxiety. Such people "crave" emotional closeness and intimacy while at the same time find it anxiety-provoking and difficult to accept.

The degree to which individuals are differentiated is a major influence on all aspects of relating to others; choosing a spouse is one example. According to Bowen (1978), people choose spouses who have similar levels of differentiation of self. People with low levels of differentiation of self have specific needs for others to feel, think and behave in certain ways. Spouses with similarly low levels of differentiation of self will most likely have chronic, unresolvable relationship problems. In commenting on this Bowen states:

> The lower the person on the scale the more he[she] makes a federal case of rejection, lack of love, and injustice, and the more he[she] demands recompense for his[her] hurts. The lower he[she] is on the scale, the more he[she] holds the other responsible for his[her] self and happiness. The lower he[she] is on the scale the more intense the ego fusions, and the more extreme the mechanisms, such as emotional distance, isolation, conflict, violence, and physical illness to control the emotion of too much closeness. In general, the lower the person on the scale, the more the impairment in meaningful communication. (p. 176)

Presently, there is little empirical research on differentiation of self, especially related to marital functioning. A study by Weinberg (1977) compared clinical (N = 20) and nonclinical (N = 20) couples on differentiation of self using a pronoun ratio scheme as a measure of this concept. This attempt at operationalizing differentiation of self is in keeping with Bowen's notion that the extent to which people are differentiated is reflected in their use of pronouns, especially "I" statements. That is, people high on differentiation of self are more likely to use the pronoun "I" when speaking about themselves while those lower on differentiation of self are more likely to speak in the second or third person using pronouns such as "you" or "it" when speaking about themselves or some aspects of their lives. This study by Weinberg found that the clinical and nonclinical couples were not significantly different on differentiation of self as measured by the pronoun ratio scheme.

Kear (1978) developed a paper-and-pencil, self-report differentiation of self scale (DOSS) designed specifically to operationalize in quantitative form this concept of Bowen theory. In his study, Kear examined the relationship between differentiation of self and marital adjustment in a nonclinical sample; marital adjustment was measured by the Locke-Wallace Marital Adjustment Test (Locke & Wallace, 1959). Married couples were found to be significantly more similar on differentiation of self than randomly paired nonmarried couples. Kear also found that more differentiated people report being better adjusted in their marriages ($r = .27$).

Kim and Merrifield (1980) factor analyzed the DOSS and found five factors: Anxiety, Emotional Distance, Familial Relationship, Emotional Maturity, and Emotional Dependency. Kim (1983) used only the Anxiety and Emotional Distance subscales in a study of 123 nonclinical couples. This study found that the more anxiety and emotional distance existing in a marriage, the greater the conflict in the marital relationship.

Parnell (1983) used the DOSS as a dependent variable in a study comparing three groups of couples who had been living together, not necessarily married, for at least one year: (1) seventeen couples who had experienced physical violence within the relationship and were currently receiving professional services of various kinds from various sources; (2) fourteen non-battering, dysfunctional couples who were in conjoint counseling; (3) fifteen couples who were not, at that time, in counseling and reported not fighting with each other. The results found that battering couples were significantly lower on the DOSS than both the nonbattering, dysfunctional couples and the control couples while the nonbattering dysfunctional couples were significantly lower on the DOSS than the control couples. These findings are consistent with Bowen's belief that differentiation of self is positively related to level of functioning.

In summary, previous research has had mixed findings regarding the differences between clinical and nonclinical spouses on differentiation of self. Though differentiation of self and marital adjustment have been examined in nonclinical spouses, clinical and nonclinical spouses have not been compared on both of these variables. This present study, therefore, examined the following hypotheses: (1) Individuals presently in marital therapy are significantly lower on differentiation of self than those not presently involved in marital therapy; (2) Individuals presently in marital therapy are significantly more likely to report having maladjusted marriages than those presently not in marital therapy; and (3) people with well differentiated selves are more likely to perceive themselves as having well adjusted marriages. The study reported in this paper combined different aspects of those by Parnell (1983) and Kear (1978) in that differences between clinical and nonclinical couples, all of whom are married to each other, were examined on both the DOSS and MAT.

METHODOLOGY

Subjects

The total sample consisted of seventy-one married couples in two different categories. The *clinical* group consisted of fifty-four spouses (twenty-seven couples) currently involved in marital therapy. These clinical spouses were recruited from human service agencies in three cities in a mid-western state. The eighty-eight spouses (forty-four couples) who comprised the *nonclinical* group were recruited from churches and friends of friends.

Instrumentation

Differentiation of Self Scale (DOSS). Differentiation of self was measured by the Differentiation of Self Scale (Kear, 1978). The DOSS consists of 41 items scored on a five-point Likert scale with a range of possible total scores of 41 to 205; a high level of differentiation of self is positively correlated with the score. Kear originally developed 72 items related to the differentiation of self concept; after pretesting and subsequent factor analysis, 41 items were retained (Kear, 1978). In a study of 219 randomly selected individuals, the 41-item DOSS was found to have an alpha reliability coefficient of .86 (Kim, 1983).

Marital Adjustment Test (MAT). Marital adjustment was measured by the Marital Adjustment Test (Locke & Wallace, 1959). This self-administered, paper-and-pencil instrument measures the extent of marital satisfaction and accommodation between a wife and husband. The MAT consists of 15 items which have weighted values. Norms for the MAT were originally established in a study of 236 married individuals (Locke & Wallace, 1959). In the study by Locke and Wallace (1959), the MAT was able to distinguish between "adjusted" and "maladjusted" couples; the MAT was also found to be a good predictor of future marital adjustment. Locke and Wallace found the MAT to be very reliable using the Spearman-Brown formula and obtaining a coefficient of .90.

Procedure

The spouses in this study were asked if they would be willing to participate in a study on marital adjustment and the self. All spouses completed identical questionnaires and were tested only once; appropriate steps were taken to ensure confidentiality. The clinical spouses were approached by their therapists and asked if they would be willing to participate in a study. Those who agreed to participate were then given the questionnaire by the therapist to complete, either at the agency or at home.

Nonclinical spouses recruited from churches were asked by their ministers if they would be willing to participate in this study. Most of these spouses met with one of the authors in groups for the administration of the questionnaire. For a few spouses recruited from churches, the questionnaire was administered by someone unrelated to the study. Other nonclinical spouses were recruited by friends of friends; this method has been used by other researchers (Ferreira, Winter & Poindexter, 1966; Parnell, 1983; Weinberg, 1977) The intermediary friend administered the questionnaire.

FINDINGS

Table 1 shows the difference between the spouses in the clinical and nonclinical groups on differentiation of self. As can be seen, the nonclinical spouses scored much higher than the clinical spouses on the DOSS; the difference was statistically significant ($p < .001$) using the t-test. The mean scores and statistical significance for these two different groups are similar to those found in previous studies which examined differences between nonclinical and clinical groups on the DOSS (Greene, Hamilton & Rolling, 1986; Parnell, 1983). This finding indicates that nonclinical spouses are more likely to be self-differentiated than clinical spouses and thus hypothesis one is supported.

Table 2 contains the findings pertaining to hypothesis two. The nonclinical spouses score on the MAT is considerably higher than the clinical spouses; a t-test found this difference to be statistically significant ($p < .001$). The spouses in the nonclinical group, as hypothesized, appear to perceive themselves as having better adjusted marriages than those in the clinical group.

Hypothesis three was examined by using a Pearson product-moment correlation. Differentiation of self and marital adjustment were found to have a positive relationship ($r = .37$) which was statistically significant at the $p < .001$ level; this finding supports hypothesis three. The coefficient of .37 appears to indicate a moderate relationship between these two variables, however, correlations with measures of general traits such as the DOSS and MAT will tend to produce lower coefficients than when specific behaviors are used in analysis (Rotter, 1975).

An additional finding was the significant, though modest, relationship between spouses on the DOSS ($r = .28$, $p > .01$). This finding

Table 1

Differences Between Clinical and Nonclinical Spouses
on Differentiation of Self

Group	N	Mean	Standard Deviation
Nonclinical	88	149.2	16.2
Clinical	54	131.2	19.6

t=5.55, p<.001

Table 2

Differences Between Clinical and Nonclinical Spouses
on Marital Adjustment

Group	N	Mean	Standard Deviation
Nonclinical	88	113.6	24.1
Clinical	53	81.5	31.7

t=6.35, p<.001

provides some support for Bowen's belief that people pick spouses who are similarly differentiated.

DISCUSSION

The findings of this study provide some support for Bowen's position that people low on differentiation of self are more likely to be maladjusted in their marriages than people higher on differentiation of self. Such a relationship between these two variables may seem self-evident to practicing clinicians, however, the science of psychotherapy requires that practice be based on more than practice wisdom.

What relevance, then, do these findings have for clinicians seeing married couples in their everyday practice?

A primary goal of Bowen marital therapy is to increase the levels of differentiation of self of the spouses. It is necessary for a clinician using a Bowen approach to marital therapy to keep the anxiety level low in the sessions with the spouses in order to facilitate the increase in differentiation of self. To achieve a low anxiety atmosphere, the marital therapist asks spouses questions which encourage them to be analytical about their marital relationship. This type of cognitive work allows spouses to keep their thinking and feeling separate which in turn reduces the tendency for them to respond reactively in habitual, problematic patterns.

To assist in reducing emotional reactivity, marital therapists using a Bowen approach may need to see spouses individually. When spouses are seen together, however, they are discouraged from talking directly to each other (Bowen, 1976). In addition, spouses are discouraged by the therapist from working directly on their relationship between sessions but rather are directed to focus on changing relationships with individuals in their respective families of origin. Much of the therapy session time consists of clients reporting on their progress vis-à-vis their family of origin and receiving further "coaching" from the therapist for continuing such work in the future.

The effort to differentiate a self in one's family of origin, and thus improve the marriage, is long-term (Kerr, 1981a, 1981b; Papero, 1983). The Bowen approach to marital therapy may initially consist of weekly sessions and later monthly ones (Aylmer, 1986). Spouses must learn the Bowen family systems theory and apply it in the process of having regular contact with family of origin members. Consequently, clients must be highly motivated in order for a Bowen approach to be effective.

What should clinicians do who are concerned about increasing spouses' differentiation of self but who do not use a Bowen approach in their clinical work? Differentiation of self, as described by Bowen, involves one's feelings, thoughts, and behaviors. In contrast to the Bowen approach, other approaches to marital therapy tend to be short term and focused on problems in the areas of feeling and/or thinking and/or behaving (Guerney, Brock & Coufal, 1986; Jacobson & Margolin, 1979; Jacobson & Holtzworth-Munroe, 1986; Todd, 1986;

Stuart, 1980). Research studies have found these briefer approaches to marital therapy to be effective. No controlled outcome studies could be found on the effectiveness of a Bowen approach with a clinical population. In a controlled study with a nonclinical population (Greene & Kelley, 1985), it was found that spouses who went through a Cognitive Relationship Enhancement Program experienced significantly greater gains on the DOSS than those who had only the Relationship Enhancement Program. Targeting change on a spouse's feelings/thoughts/behaviors as they affect the marital relationship, therefore, might be just as effective and probably more efficient in increasing differentiation of self than a pure Bowen approach.

Other marital therapy approaches and Bowen marital therapy may be more similar than different. For instance, in the Relationship Enhancement (Guerney et al., 1986), Social Learning-Cognitive (Jacobson & Holtzworth-Munroe, 1986) and Structural-Strategic (Todd, 1986) approaches the therapist is primarily a calm and supportive "coach" to the couple but puts primary emphasis specifically on the couple's relationship rather than with members of their families of origin. It may be that as spouses improve their relationship with each other, they do become more differentiated which allows them to deal more effectively with members of their families of origin which in turn allows them to deal more effectively with each other and so on. Future clinical work and research should examine more closely the possibility of this circular process of differentiating a self within the context of a marital relationship.

One factor that could have contributed to lowering scores of the clinical sample in this present study was the fact that they were in marital therapy. Marital therapy requires couples to look closely at their relationships and to experiment with new behaviors. A situation such as this in itself may result in increases in anxiety and, thus, decreases in measured levels of differentiation of self. This study did not examine the relationship between length of time in marital therapy and differentiation of self. Future research should examine the relationship between length of time in therapy, differentiation of self and marital adjustment.

Limitations in the design of this present study should be considered in the interpretation of its findings. This study did not use probability sampling and, therefore, the clinical and nonclinical groups could have been different in ways that affected the outcome on the two instruments. Since the nonclinical spouses were recruited from churches and friends of friends, they could have been higher on differentiation of self and marital adjustment than a random sample of the general population. In addition, any differences the two groups may have had on relevant personal and demographic variables were not examined. Bowen (1978) states that differentiation of self is not related to intelligence or socioeconomic levels. Previous studies have found no relationship between the DOSS and the following variables: age, level of education (Citrin, 1982; Kim, 1983), gender, marital status (Kim, 1983), length of marriage and income (Citrin, 1982). Consequently, it was not seen as necessary to obtain personal and demographic variables from the respondents in this study.

CONCLUSION

Spouses in marital therapy were found to be significantly lower in differentiation of self and marital adjustment than spouses not in marital therapy; these two variables were also found to have a moderate, positive relationship. These finding indicate that differentiation of self and marital adjustment are appropriate targets for change in marital therapy and that as one changes so should the other. Given that differentiation of self consists of important aspects of how spouses feel, think and behave, it may be that other approaches to marital therapy that are problem-focused and short-term may be just as effective, if not more so, in improving differentiation of self than a pure Bowen approach which is long-term with more vaguely defined goals. Future clinical work and research should examine this possibility.

REFERENCES

Aylmer, R.C. (1986). Bowen family systems marital therapy. In N.S. Jacobson & A.S. Gurman (Eds.), *Clinical handbook of marital therapy* (pp. 107-148). New York: Guilford Press.

Bowen, M. (1966). The use of theory in clinical practice. *Comprehensive Psychiatry, 7*, 345-374.

Bowen, M. (1976). Principles and techniques of multiple family therapy. In P. Guerin (Ed.), *Family therapy: Theory and practice* (pp. 388-404). New York: Gardner Press.

Bowen, M. (1978). *Family therapy in clinical practice.* New York: Jason Aronson.

Citrin, R.B. (1982). *The relationship between differentiation of self and interspousal perception.* Unpublished doctoral dissertation, California School of Professional Psychology.

Ferreira, A.J., Winter, W.D. & Poindexter, E.J. (1966). Some interactional variables in normal and abnormal families. *Family Process, 5*, 60-75.

Greene, G.J. & Kelley, P. (1985). Cognitive relationship enhancement: An exploratory study. *Family Therapy, XII*, 231-244.

Greene, G.J., Hamilton, N. & Rolling, M. (1986). Differentiation of self and psychiatric diagnosis: An empirical study. *Family Therapy, XIII*, 187-194.

Guerney, B.G., Jr. (1977). *Relationship enhancement: Skill training programs for therapy, problem prevention, and enrichment.* San Francisco: Jossey-Bass.

Guerney, B.G., Jr., Brock, G. & Coufal, J. (1986). Integrating marital therapy and enrichment: The Relationship Enhancement Approach. In N.S. Jacobson & A.S. Gurman (Eds.), *Clinical handbook of marital therapy* (pp. 151-172). New York: Guilford Press.

Jacobson, N.S. & Holtzworth-Munroe, A. (1986). Marital therapy: A social learning-cognitive perspective. In N.S. Jacobson & A.S. Gurman (Eds.), *Clinical handbook of marital therapy* (pp. 29-70). New York: Guilford Press.

Jacobson, N.S. & Margolin, G. (1979). *Marital therapy: Strategies based on social learning and behavior exchange principles.* New York: Brunner/Mazel.

Kear, J.S. (1978). *Marital attraction and satisfaction as a function of differentiation of self.* Unpublished doctoral dissertation, California School of Professional Psychology.

Kerr, M. (1981a). Family systems theory and therapy. In A.S. Gurman & D.P. Kniskern (Eds.), *Handbook of family therapy* (pp. 226-266). New York: Brunner/Mazel.

Kerr, M. (1981b). Bowen theory and therapy. In G.P. Sholevar (Ed.), *The Handbook of marriage and marital therapy* (pp. 143-172). New York: S P Medical & Scientific Books.

Kim, W. (1983). *The relationship of anxiety and emotional distance factors in differentiation of self and rigidity-flexibility to marital conflict.* Unpublished doctoral dissertation, New York University.

Kim, W.H. & Merrifield, P. (1980). *Replication of differentiation of self scale.* Unpublished manuscript, New York University.

Locke, H.J. & Wallace, K.M. (1959). Short marital-adjustment and prediction tests: Their reliability and validity. *Marriage and Family Living, 21*, 251-255.

Papero, D. (1983). Family systems theory and therapy. In B.B. Wolman & G. Stricker (Eds.), *Handbook of family and marital therapy* (pp. 137-158). New York: Plenum Press.

Parnell, L.A. (1983). *Fusion, differentiation of self and interpersonal perception in battering couples.* Unpublished doctoral dissertation, California School of Professional Psychology.

Rotter, J.B. (1975). Some problems and misconceptions related to the construct of internal versus external control of reinforcement. *Journal of Consulting and Clinical Psychology, 43,* 56-67.

Stuart, R.B. (1980). *Helping couples change: A social learning approach to marital therapy. New* York: Guilford Press.

Todd, T.C. (1986). Structural-strategic marital therapy. In N.S. Jacobson & A.S. Gurman (Eds.), *Clinical handbook of marital therapy* (pp. 71-105). New York: Guilford Press.

Weinberg, L.H. (1977). *Differentiation and fusion in marital relationships.* Unpublished doctoral dissertation, Temple University.

Hope for Healing in Russia:
Reflections and Epilogue

Barbara Jo Brothers

As I am putting together this volume (winter 1992), the ex-Soviet Union is trying to put together a new commonwealth from the pieces of its former self. Since the theme of this issue is one in which we explore for universal threads, my thoughts turn toward the question of universal application of psychotherapeutic principles, and, in turn, toward my summer (1991) experience. It was in Russia where a group of Russian psychotherapists and a group of American psychotherapists had converged to seek and explore the application of such principles to our two countries and cultures. As we all now know, of course, this turned out to be The Summer That Was in the Soviet Union that *was*.

Most of the major magazines which would run articles, written then, published now–after Russia's non-violent explosion into a headlong pursuit of democracy–have very cautious tones. Nobody could quite believe this was real and would last. I might not have believed so either had I not been standing on the spot as it was happening. I, too, have to agree that it could still all unravel now with economic reality's iron hand clutching those people also in the icy-cold grip of the winter in which they are living as I write these words. Faith is certainly being pressed to her edges in Moscow as those courageous and burdened people try to feed their families and provide enough heat to survive the winter. It does make an editor hesitant to publish happy, hopeful words that could look absurd as the realities shift and unwind during the months between the penning and the printing.

Those of us who were there receive letters from our Russian friends in which they almost seem to be trying to reassure *us*: "We are not starving yet." "There are many people in the world who are worse off

Correspondence to the author may be addressed to Barbara Jo Brothers, 3500 St. Charles Avenue, New Orleans, LA 70115.

and some of them live in America." These brave words were written by university professors whose diet had begun to consist only of cabbage and potatoes; milk products were no longer obtainable. They were able to celebrate Christmas when a package of dried fruit got through, intact, from friends in Switzerland.

These are psychotherapists and their families, half a globe away on the other side of the earth. They go to work everyday. They are offering courses in stress management, asking for more training in "panic disorders," etc. We try to help them keep a perspective: It is not a "disorder" if you feel panic when the temperature is 5 degrees fahrenheit and you have no fuel to heat your house. I have to wonder how much of the DSM III, reasonably, can be applied to a nation of people whose oppression dates back so many years? How "universal" are our psychiatric diagnostic categories? How complicated *is* the diagnostic process in the face of such well documented trauma? Would the paramount, overriding issue not be post-traumatic stress syndrome no matter how you cut it? How useful are such terms and concepts when you are living in an entire nation of such a syndrome? It does make a systems approach seem a more applicable choice. It does make the pursuit of health in whole *systems* seem much more important.

Our shipment of vitamins and powdered milk had arrived, sent via a contact with the medical team, Project Heart to Heart. They are so pleased, not only with the supplies, but that we *care* that much what happens to them. You can get a little depressed doing your therapy in a Moscow winter on your diet of cabbage and potatoes that your mate, a professor of economics, has stood all day in the snow to bring home.

The group to which I refer–the International Institute for Connections–has organized itself to support both the person (in the sense of the kind of emotional support human beings need) and the clinical training of each of a group of Russian psychotherapists. The roots of its history date back to connections made via the Association for Humanistic Psychology in 1983 (Hassard, 1990) and with Virginia Satir's subsequent visit to the Soviet Union in May of 1988. Based in Denver, Colorado,[1] the IIC has made a long-term commitment to maintain a connection with their sister, the Russian (ex-Soviet) Insti-

---

1. Institute for International Connections, 200 S. Sherman Street, Denver, CO 80209.

tute for Professional Development in Moscow; the commitment is to continue professional exchange for the purposes of joint professional training and the healing of our two cultures. Part of the groups' missions is to study how such healing might come about.

When we arrived last summer–which turned out to be only 10 days before the event that rocked the world–our Russian friends were all depressed, agitated, or both. With long, grim faces they met us at the gates.

"How have you been?"

"It has been very hard–but we can manage as long as there is no shooting in the streets."

The year before had seen such celebration. We had been met at the airport with bouquets of flowers. We were all intoxicated with the newness of meeting our first Russian/their first American. I treasure my own memory of standing 50 kilometers outside Moscow, on a rise in the warm sunshine, a field to my back and a small lake before me. It was my first day. Sasha had come up out of the lake, muscular and dripping in his very brief swimsuit, looking like the First Man emerging from the sea. No common language between us, he began to point to the field and flowers and give me their Russian names. It did feel, in that moment in the summer sun, as if all *were* right with the world . . .

We had all wept, smiled, embraced. It was like families, long separated, being reunited after the years of separation. We all felt related. We all fell in love. We sang, we danced.

How different it was this past year, how burdened they seemed. How difficult it had been to get organized.

When Red Square filled with the tanks on the Monday after our residential conference closed on Sunday, all that made a lot more sense.

To my own surprise, after the first two or three hours–and after the initial shock–our Russian friends had begun to express *relief* that the coup had finally come. They had feared this very kind of thing for several years. Now, at least, it was here; the ambiguity was gone. Now those elements in the government resistive to change would not only sort themselves out but out of the way of reform.

And we plunged deeply into this drama which seemed so refreshingly clear: there was no mistaking who the "bad guys" were or what they wanted. There was no mistaking what the response must be: oppose them. Flood the streets with your resistance. Challenge every soldier to examine his soul. It was personal, it was immediate. As far as I could see, it was Humanity at its finest hour. *No* violence–the word went out. Give the soldiers sandwiches, festoon their tanks with flowers. In this land run red with blood for so many generations, *nobody* wants a revolution. We will all stand together.

Even the coup leaders seem to have no stomach for killing. After the incident late Tuesday night when the three young men were accidentally killed, the tanks all began to withdraw. As if on a signal they just began to turn and leave. I got this from a man who was there. He and his therapist wife had been down at the barricades and had seen the whole thing.

The city had a six hour funeral to mourn those three young men. Their flag-draped coffins were drawn slowly through the streets where thousands of the citizens of Moscow lined those streets–to pay them honor, to step from the curbs and lay flowers on the coffins as they passed.

I had walked, the day or two before, at Yeltsin's behest–immersed in Russians, shoulder to shoulder with Russians–from the parliament building to Red Square, in celebration. Go now, Yeltsin had said to the crowd, and reclaim the Kremlin. I had then watched, from the steps of St. Basil's Cathedral, the procession carrying the enormous new/ old flag of Russia, slowly circling the square. Some unidentified Russian woman climbed to the bell tower and St. Basil's bells began to peal out the news of liberation. The sun shone for the first time in days. I do not think I would have been quite as thrilled if I had just stepped out onto the moon.

In that moment, humanity seemed like a viable enterprise.

Our experiment in Russia was an attempt to live out the basic principles at the heart of therapy as residing in the personhood of the therapist: as the person of the one encounters the person of the other. Such experiments, done internationally, make little rivulets of connections between the larger streams of the cultures represented. Not one of us who made that trip was not deeply touched. That was certainly true of the Americans. I have to believe it to be true of the Russians too, who a scant seven years ago would have been in danger by even conversing with us.

One of Virginia Satir's foundational ideas is that the first tool of the therapist is the person herself, the *person* of the therapist, searching for her/his own inner resources, making him/herself a model of congruence to facilitate authentic contact. Along those same lines, it is the *person* of the patient that must be addressed and engaged in the interaction that is known as psychotherapy. As in the case of the therapist, the patient's primary resource is also the fullness of the use of self—him/herself. Those selves less preoccupied with self *doubt* and more occupied with appropriate self *appreciation* are in a better position to make good connections with the other. This "other" may be a mate, or a child, or a co-worker–or a person of another ethnic group or nationality. The cycle then becomes a positively reinforcing one so that self-images are nurtured, rather than eroded by the contact. The "selves," enriched by the contact, then feel more inner support and are able to make the contact more honest. As honesty, accompanied by mutual respect, *is* a therapeutic interaction, people connecting with people in this manner create a context for the constructive mode to continue.

It was our premise, in our dialogue with our Russian colleagues, that application of the concept of *honoring* personhood, rather than the *using* of people–done on a large enough scale–would result in healing of both our cultures.

A week later, I saw a rare example of this respect for self and other in action and bearing fruit in the streets of Moscow. It hardly seems possible even to me, who was there, but I did *see* a city of people swarm over battalions of tanks, looking each soldier squarely in the eye, and saying, in effect: Why do this? We are a noble people. Would you shoot your mother? Your sister? Your grandfather?

This was no shouting mob. In fact, to American ears, they were strangely quiet. I think that may have a lot to do with the fact that they were mostly also terrified. A tank is a rather intimidating object even when it is parked. As I say, I walked among them too. Gingerly at first, but curiosity and wonder made me bolder when I saw little old ladies scolding their drivers as if they were naughty schoolboys.

Each Muscovite who had boarded the metro and made their way to the center of town that week had made his or her decision, on a personal level, to confront the Monster who had created [made] [was] the nightmare they had lived in for the previous 70 years. And the

Monster melted in the face of the resolve of those people who guarded, with nothing but their will and their bodies, the first president they had ever been allowed to freely elect in the entire history of their nation. In this American, witnessing those collected acts, faith in humankind was restored: it is possible for a city of people, bent on peace, to effect a peaceful outcome in an extremely dangerous situation, doggedly clinging to the principle of nonviolence, yet, *humanly* asserting their will for that peace, standing by the thousands, in the rain through the night.

I want our readership to know that among the brave citizens of the city of Moscow, there is also a brave little band of psychotherapists, struggling with how to best help their clientele under immense and prolonged stress, every family of whom carries the history of one or more people dear to them lost under the reign of Stalin. They struggle there as we struggle here: with the universal occupation of how to make relationship work–for the specific human, for the couple, for the family, and for the aggregate known as society.

The Day of Transfiguration
August 21, 1991

Russia groaned and heaved–
(Yea, of course, she has groaned and heaved for all the dark centuries . . .)
She groaned and heaved . . .
But, this time, she stood up.
And the gray-faced men rolled off her back and into the gutters;
And the men with blood in their faces stood up too–
They stood silently
They stood solidly
They stood in their fear
They stood each in their separate trembling
But they *stood*.
Not this time. This time they wouldn't melt away. This time, they
    stood;
And the tanks pushed out of hell's edges and over the brink in to
    Reality
The gray-faced men toppled over and rattled away like empty beer
    cans

While the men with the blood flowing in their veins (even as they
 trembled in their boots)
Put the flowers where the bullets had so recently been
And took those brave steps that may redeem us all.
Russia groaned and heaved and stood up.
 The home of the brave and the land of the free.

REFERENCE

Hassard, J. (1990). The AHP Soviet exchange project 1983-1990 and beyond. *Journal of Humanistic Psychology 30*(3),6-51.